Introducing Alaska

Introducing
Alaska

BY J. B. CALDWELL

Illustrated

G. P. PUTNAM'S SONS, NEW YORK

COPYRIGHT, 1947, BY J. B. CALDWELL

27977

Designed by Robert Josephy

MANUFACTURED IN THE UNITED STATES OF AMERICA

VAN REES PRESS · NEW YORK

This book is dedicated to my mother—my inspiration since babyhood, and to my wife—my further inspiration and constant companion and assistant in research and in preparing the manuscript.

ACKNOWLEDGMENTS

GRATEFUL acknowledgment is made for the following contributions to *Introducing Alaska*.

To Mr. Don L. Irwin, General Manager, Alaska Rural Rehabilitation Corporation, Palmer, Alaska, for a great deal of assistance and factual information.

To the United States Department of the Interior, Fish and Wildlife Service, Juneau, Alaska, for factual information and photographs.

To Mr. D. B. Stewart and others of his staff of the Department of Mines, Juneau, Alaska, for factual information.

To the Alaska Road Commission, Juneau, Alaska, for factual information.

To Region 10, Forest Service, United States Department of Agriculture, Juneau, Alaska, for factual information and photographs.

To Mr. Emery F. Tobin and the entire staff of the *Alaska Sportsman*, Ketchikan, Alaska, for factual information, photographs, and for checking entire manuscript.

To many other individuals, department heads, and photographers throughout Alaska who contributed generously of information and photographs.

Without your kind assistance this book could not have been written. Please accept my sincere thanks.

J. B. Caldwell

CONTENTS

FOREWORD

WHEN the Japanese landed on Attu at the extreme tip of Alaska, they accomplished one good purpose. They turned the spotlight of publicity on Alaska, and many people in the States discovered for the first time this big friendly territory of ours.

Next came reports from construction workers and thousands of armed forces personnel, of Alaska's tremendous agricultural, commercial, and recreational potentialities.

The little stream of visitors and settlers that has flowed steadily into the Territory began to rise even before the war ended, and now has assumed the aspects of a flood.

More than 350,000 people have announced their plans to go to Alaska within the next few years. Some will go there to enjoy Alaska's splendid recreational resources; others, weary of the old established communities and eager to pit themselves against frontier conditions, plan to make a home in the Territory. In this latter group are many ex-servicemen. More than four million other people have placed Alaska first on their preference list for a postwar trip, second only to Europe as a desirable place to visit.

I have done extensive research work on Alaska during the past decade, including extended personal research trips throughout the Territory. I have talked with prospectors and trappers in the hills, miners, farmers, commercial fishermen, businessmen, professional men, armed forces personnel, and government department heads.

I have fished and hunted throughout the Territory.

The vast amount of information I accumulated during that period was condensed in a magazine article and published in a series during 1945. So great was the demand for this first-hand information that the supply of the issues containing the articles was soon exhausted. A number of requests were received asking that the material be augmented by additional information and published in book form. Some of these requests were from government department heads. All of them indicated a definite need for such a book as *Introducing Alaska*.

The reader should be interested to know that every chapter in this book has been carefully checked for accuracy and approved by an Alaska expert on that particular subject, and then read a second time and approved by a well-known Alaska publisher with many years' experience in the Territory.

If you plan a hunting, fishing, or sight-seeing trip to Alaska, or if you are interested in the commercial possibilities of its timber, minerals and metals, fish, furs, industrial development, or farming and ranching, it is the purpose of this book to give you detailed information concerning each of those subjects.

J. B. Caldwell

Introducing Alaska

CHAPTER ONE

General Information

FAR to the north, where the midnight sun lights the heavens in summer and the aurora flashes its weird light across the winter sky, lies a big, rugged, boisterous country.

There, 160 acres of free land may be had for the taking; a settler may cut the straight, slender spruce and build a home, and the rich, newly cleared soil will produce abundantly.

In that new and unspoiled land men strap on their six-shooters, pick up their Winchesters, and go into the forests to hunt for the winter meat supply; and a few steps off the beaten trails are virgin forests crisscrossed with ice-cold mountain streams and dotted with crystal-clear lakes teeming with fish.

That country, once called Al-ay-ek-sa—the Great Land—by the natives, is Alaska, your frontier.

This last great frontier holds an inherent appeal to the American people whose forebears spread over a new continent a hundred years ago.

The mere mention of Alaska conjures up visions of silent expanses, towering mountains, huge glaciers, herds of big game, furs, whales, walrus, salmon, sled dogs, Eskimos, sourdoughs, gold, dance-hall queens.

In recent times vision has given way to feverish activity. The sound of ax, saw, and hammer is heard as new homes go up in the wilderness. Bulldozers roar as they push over stumps and level the land in preparation for the planting and growing of marvelous crops of produce and grain. Thriving towns are filled to overflowing with newcomers. Salmon canneries are beehives of activity. Sawmills hum. Ships and small boats shuttle up and down and across the rivers and sea channels. Cars and trucks dot the streets and highways. Airplanes zoom overhead.

And in the near-by hills the huge brown bear snorts in anger and alarm, and the wolf pack howls in protest at the intrusion.

The time has come when the American people should become better acquainted with Alaska and be able to distinguish between reality and romance, fact and fiction, so that they may know exactly what to expect in Alaska. It is remarkable that so many people otherwise well informed still prefer to believe that Alaska is a cold, inhospitable country, covered throughout the year with ice and snow, populated by Eskimos shivering in igloos heated by whale-oil lamps. This popular fallacy has prevailed since we purchased Alaska from Russia in 1867. A bitter controversy raged as to the wisdom of the purchase, and such uncomplimentary names as Walrussia, American Siberia, Zero Land, Polaria, and Icebergia were applied to Alaska by those who opposed its purchase.

Incidentally, we paid $7,200,000 for Alaska—about two cents an acre—and have already taken more than $2,500,000,000 out of it.

The first mistaken opinion about Alaska was further strengthened when gold was discovered not far from the Arctic Circle in the Fairbanks and Nome areas. Newspapers throughout the nation and the world leaped eagerly at the exciting news and headlined the struggles of those early gold seekers with stories accompanied by pictures of icy wastes.

The stories were grasped by many writers of that day, who recognized the romance and tragedy of the gold fields. Tall tales of blood-chilling experiences were written, some by authors that never ventured ten feet away from the potbellied stove and the questionable comfort of the liquor bottle.

It is cold in central and northern Alaska in winter—sometimes frightfully cold. The same is true of the Dakotas, Minnesota, northern Michigan, Montana, and other places in the States. It is also true that colder temperatures have been recorded in Montana, Wyoming, and North Dakota than have ever been recorded in Barrow, the northernmost tip of Alaska. The cold of extreme northern Alaska is tempered somewhat by the proximity of the ocean. However, some parts of interior Alaska have registered lower temperatures than anywhere in the States—about ten degrees lower.

But what a shock those believers in "Seward's Icebox" are going to get on their first trip to Alaska in summer when they approach Ketchikan's bathing beach, crowded with sun-tanned men, women, and children enjoying the excellent bathing facilities.

Mountain lakes, if not fed by mountain streams, offer comfortable bathing in summer throughout southern and southeastern Alaska. Many other towns likewise have bathing beaches; there is a beautiful beach near Juneau, and Juneau also has swimming facilities at a near-by lake; and there are beaches at Petersburg, Wrangell, and Cordova. Portions of southern Alaska have seldom known zero temperatures, and the whole of southeastern Alaska compares favorably with Meridian, Mississippi; Dallas, Texas; or Tallahassee, Florida. The lowest temperature ever recorded at Sitka was five below; at Ketchikan zero has been recorded only twice in twenty years; at Juneau, six times in twenty years. Northeastern

Alaska, almost under the Arctic Circle, has tropical temperature readings of 90 to 100 degrees in summer, and sunstroke
is not unknown. After all, the main body of Alaska is due west
of Sweden, and southeastern Alaska is due west of Scotland,
with only the northern portion of the Territory above the
Arctic Circle.

Contrary to the opinion of many people in the States, there
is year-round boat service to the whole of southeastern and
southern Alaska as far west as the Alaska Peninsula. Even
Nome has boat service until about October 15.

The mountains of south central Alaska, which follow to
some extent the contour of the southern coast, extend in a
crescent shape in an easterly-westerly direction, blocking the
frigid blasts from the Arctic; and the warm Pacific current
along the southern shore tends further to temper the southern
and southeastern portions of Alaska. Thus the average temperature in Ketchikan in January is 33 degrees above zero, and
in July 56.

The cool summer temperature is caused by ice fields and
glaciers in the near-by mountains, formed during winter when
the edge of the low barometric pressure trough—that breeder
of storms known as the Aleutian Low, which usually prevails
in the Gulf of Alaska along the southern shore—creates excessive snowfall on the southern slopes of the mountains. This
same low-pressure trough precipitates excessive rainfall along
the coast line—a maximum of about 150 inches a year in parts
of southeastern Alaska—and also contributes to the mild
winter temperatures of the area.

The total annual precipitation in the upper Yukon basin—
the area of high barometric pressure—varies locally from 5 to
14 inches. At Eagle it is about 11 inches, at Fairbanks 12
inches, at Dawson over in Canada 13 inches, and at Tanana

14 inches. The annual snowfall in this district is from 3 to 8 feet. The average precipitation in the Anchorage–Matanuska Valley area is about 15 inches. Nome has about 18 inches.

For the purpose of comparison: The extreme southeastern portion of Alaska has a low temperature in winter about equal to the north central part of Texas, with a zero spell every ten years or so. However, the mean temperature in this area during January is about ten degrees lower than north central Texas and averages a little above freezing.

The southern coast, with an average winter temperature of about 32 degrees above zero, compares in that to central Maryland, southern Illinois, and southern Kansas. However, to the northward winter temperatures become progressively more severe, and extremely cold weather is frequent in the interior basin and the Arctic region. In the Yukon and Tanana valleys the annual temperature range is pronounced, varying from an average of more than 20 degrees below zero for January in the coldest parts, to about 60 degrees above in July, or an annual range of more than 80 degrees, compared with a little more than 20 degrees in the more southern sections.

The Anchorage–Matanuska Valley area has an average winter temperature of from 13 to 24 degrees above zero, with an occasional spell of zero or lower.

Nome has an average winter temperature of about 3 degrees above zero, and a summer temperature average above 50.

Thus it is possible in Alaska to select both climate and rainfall—cold, moderate, or mild; wet, medium, or dry. And the boy who wrote home from the construction camp where he was stationed on the Alaska highway that it was the "coldest place on earth in winter and the hottest place in summer." wasn't too far off in his statement, and the soldier who wrote from the Aleutians that it was "a windy, foggy, cold, damp, and treeless place," was likewise reasonably correct for the locality. But it must be borne in mind that they were a thousand miles apart, and between them lay some 586,400 square miles of territory—one-fifth the size of the United States—with variations of climate, precipitation, forests, treeless ridges, and differences in terrain seldom found in that distance anywhere else on earth.

The Eskimo-igloo idea is likewise somewhat fanciful. It is true that there are some fifteen thousand Eskimos in Alaska, living mostly along the northern coast; but they live in houses built of lumber or driftwood, covered on both top and sides with sod. The only time they live in igloos is when they are on a winter hunt and need temporary shelter. And contrary to the usual portrayal, igloos are built of snow instead of ice—it is easier to build them of snow. When caught in a sudden winter storm, the Eskimo sometimes burrows into a snowbank, where he and his sled dogs huddle until the storm has passed.

The Eskimo home is heated with either an improvised or store-bought stove, and the temperature inside the house is usually 80 degrees or higher, even when the outside temperature is 40 or 50 below.

The Eskimo is a pleasant fellow, an expert hunter, boatbuilder, and carver, and with very little training a good mechanic. His wife is truly an artist in making skin garments. No better boot has ever been built for the north country than the Eskimo-made *mukluk*. Stitches sewed by Eskimo women in the making of this footwear are waterproof, even airproof, without treating. No machine stitching has ever equaled it. The heavy soles, where they turn up to form the lower portion of the boot, are chewed by their strong teeth to make them pliable.

Long before the advent of the white man, the Eskimo made

artificial fishing lures similar to our manufactured lures, and used sinew leaders. He also made very satisfactory goggles, fish nets of skin and sinew, raincoats of seal guts, rope from spruce roots, and skis of whalebone covered with the skin of the hair seal. Many examples of these skillfully made articles are on exhibit at the Territorial Museum in Juneau.

Eskimos are very fond of sweets, enjoy smoking, get drunk too easily, and some of them are regular card sharks. It is noteworthy that the Eskimo did not suffer tooth decay until the sugars and starches came into his diet, introduced by the white man.

They do not rub snow on a frozen cheek or ear, but instead they apply a warm hand to the frozen part.

Eskimo mothers along the coast carry their babies inside their own fur garments, and when the baby becomes overheated, they take him out, absolutely naked, deposit him on a skin spread on the snow, even when the thermometer is far below zero, and leave him there for half a minute or so until he is cooled off.

The Eskimo is fast becoming modernized, adopting many of the white man's ways of living. Some of this modernization produces unusual contrasts. It is not unusual to see a skin boat put-putting along under the power of an outboard motor, although the construction of these boats has not changed for a thousand years or more.

Many circumstances point to the Eskimo's oriental origin. Tales of dragons, tigers, and other oriental lore, handed down from generation to generation, give credence to the supposition that Eskimos originally came from the Orient. Their belief in transmigration of the soul or reincarnation of the soul in an animal likewise traces back to oriental origin. Chinese coins several centuries old have been found in Eskimo ruins. One coin of great significance is the large temple coin that was dug up at Knik in 1913, together with a stone lamp of rare and unusual design. The coin was determined to be of the Chow dynasty (A.D. 700). These articles are in the Territorial Museum in Juneau.

The Eskimo's personal appearance certainly does not belie the supposition of oriental kinship. And yet, strangely enough, the earliest middens, such as that at Ipiutak (two thousand years old) bear no evidence of Chinese culture.

In addition to some fifteen thousand Eskimos, Alaska has about an equal number of Indians. Racial subdivisions include the Athapascan, Chimmesyan, Haida, Tlingit, and Chilcat. The Aleuts, who once numbered thousands on Kodiak and the Aleutian Islands, have suffered a startling decline in population since the white man came among them. However, census figures indicate that the total native population has just about held its own since 1900.

These native peoples are granted a great many special privileges by the government in the killing of game and taking of fish. Some are employed by the government in seal hunting and preparing the hides; others are employed by the canneries in season; still others follow their ancient vocations—hunting, fishing, and trapping. Some Indians of southeastern Alaska are expert wood carvers, and their totem poles are viewed as works of historical art.

Intermarriage of whites and Indians or whites and Eskimos is not uncommon, and there are many half-breeds throughout Alaska. Not all of them are the offspring of legitimate marriages, for the moral code of the Eskimo and Indian peoples is, not surprisingly, somewhat different from ours. Nor have the white people that have come to Alaska always upheld the moral standard of their race.

The tuberculosis ratio among Eskimos and Indians is some-what higher than among whites. There are approximately four thousand reported cases in Alaska at present among both natives and whites, which is less than 5 per cent of the total population. Some families—even tribes—have a much higher percentage than that, and the situation is critical enough so that additional appropriations have been made to combat further inroads of the disease. However, exaggerated esti-mates made by uninformed writers that up to 90 per cent of the natives suffer the ravages of tuberculosis are not substan-tiated by facts. A recent survey among a group of natives on Kodiak revealed that about 20 per cent were affected. The crowded, overheated conditions that prevail among Eskimos and the poorly balanced diet and living habits of some Indian tribes existing under primitive conditions are said to be contributing factors to the higher tuberculosis ratio among natives.

On the basis of the 1940 census, which showed Alaska's total population as 72,524, and if Alaska's phenomenal growth since 1940 is taken into account, undoubtedly the population of the Territory is now nearing the 100,000 mark, of which 50,000 to 70,000 are white. They follow commercial fishing, mining, lumbering, trapping, agriculture, and merchandising for a livelihood. Federal, territorial, and municipal employees make up a goodly proportion. An estimated one third of the permanent white population is grouped in the extreme south-eastern part of the Territory.

Although the last census gave Alaska only one permanent inhabitant to each eight square miles, it is the fastest growing division under the American flag. From 1930 to 1940 Alaska's population increased 22.3 per cent. This growth was exceeded by only two states, Florida and New Mexico. Since 1940, however, Alaska has outstripped those two states, or any other part of America.

Most outsiders visiting Alaska for the first time expect to find frontier conditions and dress somewhat similar to that in vogue in the States a century ago. They are amazed to learn that the people in the towns throughout Alaska are more sophisticated, better dressed, and better educated than those in most towns of like size in the States. Nearly every woman to be seen on the streets of Alaska's towns has the latest hair-do and is dressed in good taste and in the height of fashion. Men wear conventional business clothes, and only occasionally, except during the commercial fishing season when they are seen frequently, are boots and rough clothes, usually associated with frontiers, in evidence. Large white hats, laced boots, and working clothes, so common in some of the States, are conspicuous by their absence on the streets of Alaska's towns.

Hotels and eating places that compare favorably with those to be found in cities of several hundred thousand population in the States are common throughout Alaska. Neon and fluorescent lighting enhances the attractiveness of many cafés and restaurants, and whole towns are lighted at night with a Christmas-like brilliance.

Modern conveniences are enjoyed by Alaska people even in some of the very small towns. The little town of Chitina with perhaps a dozen inhabitants has its own electric lighting and sewer systems.

Alaskans find much more time to play than do people in the States. Fishing, hunting, hiking, skiing, skating, boating, and photography are the principal recreational activities. Baseball is played in summer, and a midnight game under the light of the midnight sun is an annual affair. Owing to difficulties of transportation, football has not gained a foothold in the Territory, and a game at Fairbanks in 1945 between two teams of servicemen was said to be the first football game ever played in that portion of Alaska.

Hiking and packing all manner of things on their backs into remote places are a sort of mania with Alaskans. They pack everything, even prefabricated houses, into out-of-the-way places, and recently the Ketchikan Ski Club members packed a hundred-pound heating stove up a tortuous trail three miles to their cabin near the summit of Deer Mountain above Ketchikan. Two-by-fours strapped to each side of the stove furnished convenient handles, and their only expressed regret was that they did not have a large-sized pack board so that the stove could be strapped onto it and each one, individually, could enjoy the pleasure of packing the stove part way up. This unusual passion for pack boards manifested by Alaskans is undoubtedly traceable to the inaccessibility of many near-by recreation spots, which can be visited only by those possessing strong legs and strong backs as all equipment must be packed in. And Alaskans have learned to like it.

Alaska is noted for its abundance and variety of wild life. Among the most sought-after game and fur animals are moose, mountain sheep, mountain goats, deer, caribou, bears, minks, martens, land otters, weasels, foxes, lynx, muskrats, beavers, wolves, coyotes, wolverines, marmots, and squirrels.

Steelhead, cutthroat, rainbow, eastern brook, and Dolly Varden trout and grayling abound in the streams and lakes, and salmon, halibut, herring, cod, clams, crabs, and various other commercial fish are taken in profusion off the coasts.

The menu of a wild-game dinner in Anchorage recently consisted of caribou, mountain goat, moose, porcupine, bear, ptarmigan, grouse, ducks, geese, rabbit, and salmon, as well as wild berries and other ordinary foods.

The lowly porcupine, which has no defense against its enemies except its rather formidable quills, is considered to be a good food animal in Alaska. However, it is seldom hunted commercially or for sport, as it is the one source of meat supply that may be obtained with only a club by those that become lost or stranded without firearms in the vast uninhabited portions of Alaska. Porcupines make cunning pets, and unless frightened or excited, the porcupine keeps its vicious quills laid flat, and it may be handled with impunity if one uses caution.

Alaskans that hunt regularly each fall to augment their regular meat supply are usually successful in their efforts to bag a moose, caribou, or deer, which they do not hunt for trophies, such as wide antler spreads, but rather for younger animals with tender flesh.

Bears are among the most numerous, interesting, and attractive of Alaska's wild life. The huge Alaska brown bear, the largest carnivorous animal on earth, sometimes attains a weight of more than 1,500 pounds, yet the newborn cubs of this gigantic mother weigh approximately a pound and are about the size of a rat.

There are some twenty-eight species of brown and grizzly bears in Alaska, to say nothing of the black and glacier bears. It often takes an expert to distinguish between the different species, as they vary greatly in color and appearance.

Bears are notoriously unpredictable creatures, and nowhere else in the animal kingdom is individuality and personality more marked. As a rule they prefer to run away rather than do battle with man, but the exceptions to the rule are too often fatal to the human adversary. It is a good plan to consider all bears dangerous; however, black bears seldom attack a man except when wounded or in defense of their young.

They are considered nuisances by many Alaskans, because of their habit of breaking into houses and caches. It is not unusual for a bear to enter a home during the owner's absence and wreak hundreds of dollars' damage. They have a propensity for destroying and eat nearly anything they find, including such dainties as soap and silver polish.

Unusual encounters with bears are common in Alaska. A woman in southeastern Alaska recently had the exciting experience of stepping on a live bear as she backed down a steep place in the trail carrying a small outboard motor. Dan Noonan, prominent Alaska traveling man, reports that a bear slapped him between the shoulders as he leaned over to remove a gravel from his shoe. The bear did not follow up the attack, and Dan left there in a hurry, without his shoe. An army sergeant had a fist fight with a bear not long ago when it swam out into the water where he was bathing. The bear caught a few lefts and rights to the nose, and the sergeant went to the hosptial for chest lacerations.

Fishermen along Alaska streams attach tin cans filled with pebbles to their belts so that they will not suddenly come upon a bear. Bears have poor eyesight, but their ears and noses are keen, and any unusual noise such as that made by the pebbles in the can will disturb them and cause them to move on, even on a windy day when the man scent is wafted away from them.

Bears from isolated sections often cross a mountain and walk unconcernedly into a town in Alaska. A large brown bear came into the village of Chitina not long ago, walked up the main street and looked from side to side at the new and interesting sights, turned at the corner in the heart of the village, and meandered slowly off into the near-by mountains. The villagers watched the bear cautiously from behind closed doors, but it was unmolested, as it showed no belligerency and did no property damage.

Every year a few people in Alaska are attacked by bears and frightfully mauled, sometimes killed. A bear has been known to attack a man in an unusual manner, using neither teeth nor claws in the initial attack. It simply runs the man down by hitting him a terrific blow with its chest. When he is down, the bear usually worries him as a terrier worries a rat, and desists only when it thinks the man is dead. Bears do not eat human flesh—at least no authentic firsthand accounts are available of bears eating human beings—but they do eat almost every other kind of flesh, including other bears. Black bears usually avoid islands and other places where browns and grizzlies predominate, although some areas are common to all species. Black bears display uneasiness and give ground readily at the approach of one of the larger species.

Many of Alaska's fur bearers, including wolves, feed on lemmings, small tailless rodents that undergo cycles of over- and underpopulation. When their range becomes over- crowded, these tiny creatures emigrate in millions onto the ice of the Arctic Ocean, never to be seen again. It is presumed that all of them drown when the ice breaks up in the summer. This emigration to the sea is noted also in the central mountains of Scandinavia. Some scientists claim that age-old instincts force the animals toward islands that once existed out in the sea but have long since disappeared. This claim may well be true of the Alaska lemming, for it is a generally accepted theory that Alaska was at one time joined to the Asiatic mainland.

Wild life in Alaska has not yet retreated wholly before the encroachment of civilization. Recently a plane, taxiing for a take-off on the water near Petersburg, ran into something on the surface—something that brought it to an abrupt stop. Upon investigation, the pilot was dumfounded to see a large whale quietly swimming away, apparently unperturbed at having its nap so rudely disturbed.

It is not unusual in Alaska for a hunter to return home from an all-day hunt in distant fields, to bag a moose, deer, or bear in or near his own front yard.

Some twenty deer were observed recently near the city limits of Ketchikan beside the footpath that leads to the top of Deer Mountain.

A hunter parked his car near the end of the bridge across the channel from Juneau last season, walked a short distance up the mountain, and bagged a deer within sight and sound of the capital city, and many deer are killed in that same vicinity and near other Alaska towns every season.

Both wolves and coyotes are said to be on the increase throughout Alaska, and while wolves are known to destroy large numbers of mountain sheep, deer, caribou, and even moose, some doubt appears to exist in the minds of those that have made a careful study of the wolf's place in nature's planning that its depredations are so much of a factor in game depletion as heretofore accepted conclusions indicated. Overpopulation of mountain sheep, for instance, leads to their starvation during extremes of snowfall over their ranges, whereas a wolf-thinned population has a much higher survival ratio.

Nearly all Alaska animals, even the wolves, die of epizootic diseases—diseases which affect nearly all of one species, comparable to epidemics among humans—when their numbers increase until their range is overcrowded. Some argue that these epizootic diseases among game animals do not recur so frequently among wolf-thinned herds. Wolves pull down and destroy the sick and the weak, which no doubt prevents to some extent the spread of disease to the healthy ones. But they also destroy many young healthy animals and have been known to approach a herd from both sides, pass up the stragglers, and pull down the strongest animals—the leaders—thus creating confusion and chaos among the others so that many kills are easily made.

Undoubtedly man's advent into the picture upsets nature's planning, and it is doubtful that both wolves and man can exploit the herds without depleting them to dangerous, rather than beneficial numbers. That is why Alaska has inaugurated the present high bounties on coyotes and wolves. (See Appendix for bounties.)

Wolves in Alaska do some rather remarkable things in connection with their gregarious habits: It is not unusual for a pair of wolves with pups to have several companions of both sexes which assist in bringing up the family. They bring food to the mother wolf while she keeps watch over the pups, and later when the pups are older, bring food to both mother and pups. They are exceedingly friendly with one another, and the pups romp at will over and around the older wolves as they doze near the den. Later, the pair of wolves with their pups, and with the companions, make up a pack of ten to twenty, and all hunt together.

In deep snow one wolf goes ahead and breaks trail, and the others follow in its footsteps. They are said to alternate in the matter of trail breaking so that the entire burden does not fall on the original leader.

Wolves are cunning, and coyotes are especially hard to trap. An armed hunter may tramp for days in a district alive with wolves without seeing one; but let him go into the woods unarmed and he is likely to find himself entirely surrounded by wolves. Although they seldom attack a human being, they seem to derive considerable pleasure from eying him hungrily from a few yards away.

Foxes are scattered widely throughout Alaska, with red, blue, silver, black, and cross predominating. Some Alaska foxes have learned to use ice floes to ferry from one island to another. The remarkable thing about that is that it necessitates observance of the direction of tide flows.

The wolverine—the toughest animal in proportion to size in the north country—is shunned by other animals, not only because of its skunklike odor but also because of its ferocity. A wolf over twice its size has been known to come out second best in combat with a wolverine, and even large bears avoid the woodland toughie. A Dr. Huffman caught a wolverine in a number-two steel trap, which the wolverine proceeded to take apart piece by piece, laying the parts out in the snow like a mechanic. Then the wolverine dragged a hundred-pound moose head, which had been used for trap bait, over two miles up a mountain, and the wolverine weighs considerably less than half that much.

The wolverine is a noted trap robber, killing and tearing to pieces with maniacal fury animals caught in traps, if it finds them before the trapper runs his line.

Ducks, geese, and other migratory birds nest by the millions in Alaska. Thousands of square miles of uninhabited tundra areas provide sanctuary for these annual visitors.

Some sea birds are said to lay their eggs on volcanic islands where the heat from below helps to incubate them.

Like the great Alaska brown bear, many other animals of Alaska grow to unusual size. Mountain goats sometimes reach the great weight of 350 pounds. Salmon have been caught weighing over 100 pounds, and the king crab of the Bering Sea frequently measures 6 feet from toe to toe. Arctic hares weigh almost 20 pounds, and furnish both food and fur for the Eskimos.

A beaver pelt of more than 67 inches, length and breadth combined, is often taken. Such large skins are called blankets and sometimes bring as much as fifty dollars.

Seals are plentiful along much of Alaska's coast line. Fur seals, slaughtered only under rigid control of the United States Government, are the only commercially valuable members of the seal family, although other members furnish skins and food for the native peoples of Alaska.

Six thousand sea lions are said to inhabit the rookery of Sugar Loaf Islands off southeastern Alaska.

Reindeer, imported into Alaska at the turn of the century, have come to play a considerable part in the far-northern economy. Reindeer meat is the mainstay of the menu from Nome northward. Neglect, poor management, and remote government control are said to be contributory causes of the present great depletion of the herds.

Not all Alaska animals migrate southward in winter. Some remain in their usual habitat in the far north, others even migrate northward, and there is said to be considerable animal and marine life even near the North Pole.

It sometimes rains fish on the St. Lawrence Islands off western Alaska. They vary in size from small fingerlings up to ten pounds. For a long while nobody could explain this strange phenomenon, until a scientist finally expounded the theory that fish are frozen in the ice; the tremendous pressure of the ice floes breaks the ice into small pieces; strong winds tear the fish from these pieces of ice and hurl them onto the shore. The islanders do not question the source but grab up buckets

Bathing beaches are common throughout Southeastern Alaska, and even at Fairbanks residents enjoy summer diversions at near-by Harding Lake. (*Copyright Department of the Interior*)

Hunting is unexcelled in Alaska where there are the largest moose to be taken anywhere. (*Copyright The Alaska Sportsman*)

Caribou, whose horns are much sought after for trophies, are
the most plentiful of Alaska's fine meat animals. (*Copyright The
Alaska Sportsman*)

The dream of every big-game hunter is the Alaska brown bear, largest carnivorous animal on earth. (*Copyright Forest Service*)

Alaska mountain sheep offer excellent sport. (*Copyright The
Alaska Sportsman*)

A fisherman's skill is taxed to the utmost to bring to gaff a big king salmon such as this forty-pounder. (*Copyright Frank R. Geeslin*)

Lake trout are of extraordinary size even in well-fished Alaskan waters. (*Copyright Harry T. Becker*)

Alaska's streams are teeming with trout that often do not fit the creel. (*Copyright The Alaska Sportsman*)

Fish, like this, can be caught from the docks of Alaska's
coastal towns as fast as the fisherman's hook hits the water.

and baskets, and braving the hazard of being slapped in the face by a falling fish, they gather up the unusual harvest.

Literally Alaska is not a land flowing with milk and honey. Milk is hard to get in many districts, and it is said that there are no wild honeybees in Alaska. However, hornets are native to the Territory, and nests are occasionally encountered. Some bees have been imported into Alaska during summer, and produce bountiful crops of honey from the many varieties of Alaska wild flowers, but they do not survive the cold winters of central Alaska and do not thrive in the wet winters of southeastern Alaska.

The lowly muskrat is one of the principal fur bearers of Alaska. Along the Kuskokwim River schools close, and everyone goes "ratting" in season. Muskrats not only furnish bread-and-butter income, but their flesh is an important food. It is tender and delicately flavored.

It was gold that attracted people to Alaska in vast numbers from 1898 through the ensuing decade, and indeed, the gold rushes to the Klondike, Fairbanks, and Nome areas were the most spectacular migrations of modern times. Although the stories that came from the gold seekers served to build up false impressions of Alaska, many of them are literally true. Gold was so plentiful in some of the original placer mines that children could pan out several dollars' worth with their bare hands in a short time. There was no janitor problem in some of the old-time gambling houses and saloons! Every crack and cranny of the floor was scrupulously cleaned and the dirt panned for gold, which produced as much as fifty dollars' worth a day. When the old buildings and sidewalks of the famous gold metropolises burn, there's a miniature stampede to pan the ashes.

Weather and rainfall produce some peculiarities in Alaska.

When spruce forests burn, the burned-over land is usually overgrown by birch or alder. Most of southern and southeastern Alaska is heavily forested, while portions of the Aleutians of like temperature and elevation are treeless. This condition is brought about by prevailing winds, which blow the tree seeds away from the treeless portions.

Corn, peaches, apples, and other field crops and fruits that produce in colder areas in the States do not produce so abundantly in Alaska; while at the same time potatoes, mustard crops, and berries from the same regions in the States produce more abundantly in Alaska.

There is practically no darkness from June 15 to July 10 throughout central and northern Alaska, and from mid-December to January 10 the sun struggles above the horizon for only a couple of hours. From the tops of the ridges the sun may be seen at midnight in summer in the central and northern portions of the Territory, and here also one may witness the unusual spectacle of a 1:00 P.M. sunrise late in December. The summer days are not quite so long and the winter nights are shorter in southeastern Alaska, although eighteen hours or more of sunshine may be enjoyed throughout the whole of Alaska during the growing season.

Even in the north country where the winter nights are so long, it isn't dark at night. The snow on the ground, the stars, moon, and aurora often combine to create enough light on clear nights to enable one to travel about without a light. No more beauty or solitude can be enjoyed anywhere else on earth than in north central Alaska on a still, crisp, starry winter night.

Outsiders particularly are warned of sudden storms that arise on the large lakes of interior Alaska—fearsome and dangerous things, as many can verify who have been caught out in them in a small boat. They strike without warning, sending mountainous waves crashing onto rugged shores. Native Alaskans travel many unnecessary miles hugging shore lines rather than risk being caught in open water.

Unusual gusts of wind, sometimes reaching a velocity of fifty miles an hour, play havoc with small craft along Alaska's southern and southeastern coast, causing many small boats to break their moorings, which have to be chased down by the Coast Guard. These winds come and go quickly like a whirlwind in a dry country.

Huge glaciers and ice formations that occur throughout southern and southeastern Alaska are a source of much interest to Alaska visitors. The lower end of most glaciers retreats, but some advance. Mendenhall, near Juneau, a much visited glacier, is a good example of a retreating glacier. Columbia is an advancing glacier.

Sea ice becomes less salty with age. One-year-old ice may be melted and used for drinking water, although slightly brackish. Two-year-old ice is almost as sweet as rainwater. During summer months in the Arctic, fresh-water pools form atop the salt-water ice, from which the Eskimos make their strong tea when walrus hunting. And nowadays they brew it over pocket-size gasoline stoves.

The Arctic does not always claim as its victims those that are accidentally dunked into the icy water and do not have an opportunity to change clothes immediately. One rugged Alaskan fell through a soft place in the ice up to his armpits, with the thermometer at 20 below, walked eight miles before he could change clothes, and suffered not even so much as a sniffle. Discretion forbids recommending any such strenuous manner of thwarting Arctic cold, and an immediate change of clothing and warmth still is recommended in case of such an accident.

The mosquito and other insect menace in Alaska has been exaggerated. It is true that there are millions of mosquitoes in portions of Alaska during a short period in late spring and early summer each year, and "no-see-ums," "white-sox," and other pestiferous flying insects are bothersome to some extent until late fall, but they are a definite menace to outdoor enjoyment for only a couple of months throughout most of Alaska.

Many people are surprised to learn that few houses or hotels in Alaska have screens. Alaska insects seem to avoid entering an opening where the interior is darker than outside. The white-sox—a small vicious fly with white legs—avoids entering any sort of door or window. Even in localities where hundreds of them may be flying around your face, if you step into a car or a house with the windows open, few of the pests will enter. Outside campers in Alaska require mosquito netting, even head nets and gloves when they go into the brush in spring and early summer. That is likewise true in many districts in the States.

In most southeastern Alaska towns the steep sidewalks have cleats on them to prevent slipping when iced, as many towns are built on mountainsides. Some houses have entrances from the second or third story at street level, and a person enters the house at the top of the stairs and goes down instead of entering at the bottom and going upstairs.

Hay fever is almost unknown in Alaska, owing to the absence of ragweed and other highly irritating, pollen-producing plants. A few people are allergic to spruce, however.

There are no poisonous snakes in Alaska; therefore the old excuse for carrying large supplies of the traditional "snake bite" medicine on fishing and hunting trips is no good. However, Alaskans do not seem to need an excuse. Liquor is plentiful and is one commodity that is cheaper in Alaska than in the States.

Alaska people like dogs more than outsiders do, and the towns are alive with dogs of all breeds, colors, and sizes. Even Alaska boats provide accommodations for dogs, meals included, and the fare is about 6 per cent of the regular fare for human beings. Some hotels bar them, but otherwise there seem to be no enforced regulations affecting them.

The mighty Yukon River of fact and fiction rises almost within sight of the Pacific Ocean, flows away in a northwesterly direction for a thousand miles, just crossing the Arctic Circle, then turns southwest and flows twelve hundred miles back to the Pacific side, into the Bering Sea. The Yukon is navigable for almost its entire length. It and its tributaries, the Tanana, the Koyukuk, and other streams, form the summer life line of the interior.

A large betting pool on when the ice will go out of the Yukon—the day, hour, and minute—is a feature of much speculation, participated in by nearly everybody in Alaska. The lucky guesser wins a sizable fortune. Many other smaller pools on temperature and other weather and rainfall fluctuations draw a number of participants in the towns of Alaska.

The radio is the principal means of communication throughout large portions of Alaska, and the airplane the principal means of travel to remote regions. There are more airplanes in Alaska per capita than anywhere else on earth, and the most primitive people of the north are quite casual in the use of the airplane, civilization's most spectacular offering.

A saleslady travels by air throughout Alaska, visiting many

out-of-the-way places and taking orders for nearly everything from face powder to gunpowder.

The old and the new meet in extraordinary contrast in Alaska. While observing the comings and goings of airplanes, busy in the traffic of the Territory, one may have to hold his nose to avoid the stench of decomposed prehistoric mammoth flesh from some hitherto icebound river bed that has recently caved and thawed.

Archaeologists believe that at some time in the future, a portion or the complete remains of a Folsom man, of some fifteen thousand years' antiquity, will be unearthed from his frozen tomb by such a cave-in. Folsom arrow points, intermingled with wood ashes and other deposits, have been found in Alaska, confirming the opinion of many archaeologists that America was first settled by Asiatics who crossed into Alaska when it was connected to Asia by land.

It is only three miles from Little Diomede Island, an American possession, to Big Diomede, the eastern beginning of the Soviet Union. East Cape on the Siberian mainland is only fifty-five miles from Cape Prince of Wales on Seward Peninsula. The international date line runs between Little Diomede and Big Diomede Islands, and if a person looks from Little Diomede on Monday, he is looking into Tuesday on Big Diomede.

With recently constructed roads and airplane landing fields, our vast northern territory bids fair to become the mecca of the new world for hunters, fishermen, sight-seers, and prospective settlers. The grandeur of its superb fiords, magnificent glaciers, lofty snow-capped mountains, wooded hills, mirror-like lakes, and rushing streams will delight the sight-seer and camera fan. Its abundance of fish and wild life will lure the sportsman. Its tremendous resources of timber and minerals will invite outside capital. The fertility and productivity of its farmland will bring in many new settlers.

And these are only a few of the many attractions which are bringing thousands to Alaska, your frontier.

CHAPTER TWO

Hunting

THE huge Alaska brown bear is one of the outstanding big-game animals of Alaska, and the most sought-after as a trophy. Specimens have been taken with skins eleven and one-half feet square, and with skulls that measure some nineteen inches in length by twelve inches in width. Monarch of the north woods, this monster gives ground only to man and his high-powered rifle, and that grudgingly.

It is found in considerable numbers on the Alaska and Kenai peninsulas of southwestern Alaska and near-by Kodiak Island; on Chichagof, Admiralty, and Baranof Islands off the southeastern coast; and on portions of the southern and southwestern mainlands. And since the sale of brown and grizzly bear hides was prohibited by federal law several years ago, they have gradually increased in numbers. The population of coastal brown bears is now placed at about 8,500.

The grizzly, close cousin to the brown bear and next in importance to the brownie as a trophy, covers a wider range, and roams a vast area along the salmon streams of the coast and among the mountain ranges of the central and northern parts of the Territory. Outstanding trophies have a skin measurement of over nine feet square, and a skull measurement of approximately seventeen inches in length by eleven inches in width. There are an estimated ten thousand of this species in Alaska.

Neither the brownie nor the grizzly is averse to the killing and eating of livestock, and there are portions of the mountainous areas in Alaska where livestock cannot be permitted to run at large because of the depredations of grizzlies. At one time brown bears killed so many cattle that they discouraged the raising of cattle on Kodiak.

As they appear in the forests and on the flats, there is a remarkable similarity in appearance of the brown and grizzly bears, but under close examination differences are noted in the color, claws, skull, and teeth. The pelage of the brownie is darker in color, with less admixture of golden or silver-tipped hairs, and his color is more uniform. On Admiralty Island is to be found the Shiras brown bear, which is almost coal black. Brown bears sometimes resemble more closely the grizzly than others of their own species, and it often takes an expert to distinguish between them.

Bears emerge from hibernation in April or May, and mate every other year. The mating season is in June. Grasses, roots, berries, and salmon during the salmon runs are the chief food supply of coastal bears. Interior grizzlies augment their diet with marmots and ground squirrels.

The hibernation period begins in October or November, and one to four cubs are born in January or February. Hunting is best from the latter part of April to the middle of May, and in the month of October.

Black bears are so numerous and they cover such a vast area —three fifths of the land area of Alaska—that nature seems to have outdone itself in the number of these beasts. They are found in every part of Alaska except on the Alaska Peninsula and in the extreme western part. They barely fall into the classification of a game animal in Alaska, and except for a limited area, there is no closed season and no limit on them.

Black bears are variously classified by the people of Alaska from downright nuisances to good-natured, amusing specimens of wild life. They, too, often turn killer, and not long ago three cows were killed in one pasture near Palmer in the Matanuska Valley by a black bear.

Trophies of the black bear are easily obtained, and the largest skins measure nearly eight feet square, with skulls approximately fourteen inches long by ten inches wide. Few people in Alaska value either the skin or flesh of the black bear, but nonresident hunters usually take several skins as trophies when hunting in the Territory. There are some 75,000 of them in Alaska, and it is unusual for anyone to travel any great distance, even on the highways, without seeing one or more of them.

The Alaska moose is next in order to the bears in interest to hunters. It is the largest of the deer family on earth, the bulls attaining a weight of more than 1,400 pounds. They often have an antler spread of 70 inches, with palm spread of 15 to 18 inches, and with upwards of twenty points to the side.

Moose range over 240,000 square miles—almost half of the Territory—including all of the mainland, except the extreme western and northern portions, and the Alaska Peninsula. The largest concentration and the largest antlers are found throughout the Kenai Peninsula in the southern portion of the Territory. The largest specimens are found on the Kantishna and upper Kuskokwim rivers immediately north of the Alaska Range.

The nonresident hunter is faced with his first mental and legal hazard in the killing of these huge beasts—the problem of what to do with the great quantity of fine-flavored and highly nutritious meat, after he has obtained the sought-after trophy of the wide-spreading antlers. Surely every sportsman in America revolts at the idea of killing for trophies only. And while it is a comparatively simple matter, with the assistance of a guide, to have the trophies of both bear and moose prepared and shipped, it is something else again when the matter of handling 750 to 1,000 pounds of meat intrudes itself into the picture.

There is a wanton destruction clause in the Alaska game regulations, as follows:

> Any person killing a deer or other wild food animal within the Territory of Alaska, with intent to wantonly destroy said animal and without making every effort to have such animal utilized for food, shall be guilty of a misdemeanor, and upon conviction thereof, shall be punished by a fine not exceeding five hundred ($500) dollars or imprisoned not exceeding six months.

Resident hunters are prone to pass up a kill in an inaccessible region, and as mentioned before, have long since ceased hunting for trophies.

The outside hunter must take this meat factor into account and make a special effort to insure that his kill is near enough to a water outlet, road, or trail, or in the vicinity of an Indian village or other settlement, or near the home of a settler, so that the meat from his kill may be utilized. The guide will assist him in the matter of meat disposal. (See Appendix in back of book for regulations governing export of game.)

It is perhaps true that more moose—and the same is true of other animals—die of starvation, predators, and epizootic diseases with which they are stricken than are killed by hunters; still, this natural tendency to keep down overproduction does not lessen the obligation of the hunter in the matter of meat utilization, and is not an encouragement to wanton slaughter.

The caribou, an excellent meat animal, which attains a maximum weight of five to six hundred pounds, is unquestionably the most abundant big-game animal in Alaska, numbering upwards of a million. Their antlers, with a spread of nearly sixty inches, and with a beam to the right and left nearly as much as the spread, with brow tines of some twenty inches on each side, and with fifteen to eighteen points to the side, make a beautiful trophy and are much sought after.

There are several caribou species, both mountain and barren-ground types, which include the Stone, Grant, Osborne, and the Point Barrow caribou, as well as the McGuire. This last-named species occurs along the Alaska-Yukon boundary of eastern Alaska, whereas other types are found among the higher plateaus of the Alaska and contiguous ranges in the central portion, and they are supported in great numbers on the Brooks Range north of the Arctic Circle. The Grant variety is found also on the Alaska Peninsula and the Unimak Island of southwestern Alaska.

Sitkan black-tailed deer, small editions of their southern cousins in the States, are abundant in southeastern Alaska and certain islands in Prince William Sound of southern Alaska. When full-grown, the Sitkan deer weighs about 120 pounds. And maybe he was made small on purpose, for it would take a miracle to transport a 250-pound blacktail out over the difficult terrain the Sitkan deer inhabits.

There is little need to tell the experienced hunter that these fine meat animals are seldom sought for their trophies only, as the oft-told—and oft-written—tales of the herculean struggles of hunters to transport freshly killed deer out of remote regions—piggy-back and otherwise—attest to the value placed upon venison steaks and roasts. A hunter that ordinarily will scrupulously avoid overtaxing or overstraining himself will ofttimes tax his physical resources literally to the point of utter and complete exhaustion to bring out a deer. And not a little of the hunter's anxiety to bring the deer into camp or transport it home is pride. He just naturally likes to bring in the bacon.

The shaggy white mountain goat, bewhiskered old gentleman of the high coastal mountain cliffs and crags, is so well protected in its difficult habitat that there is little danger of its being hunted to extermination. There are an estimated 12,500 of these animals in the higher mountains of southeastern Alaska, and in the Chugach Range and the Kenai Peninsula of southern Alaska. The head with horns and the skin of these animals are much prized as trophies, and the meat of a young mountain goat is of good texture and excellent flavor. It has very little of the "goat taste."

These fine animals tax the endurance and ingenuity of even the most hardy hunter, and he should possess unusual stamina and ability if he would seek them in their mountain fastnesses.

Mountain sheep of Alaska, said to be the only white sheep in the United States or its possessions, number some forty thousand. They have a considerably wider range than mountain goats and are to be found in the Alaska Range of south central Alaska, in parts of the Chugach and Kenai Mountains of southern Alaska, and in the Brooks Range of northern Alaska, where the largest herds in North America live. They are also plentiful in the Nutzotin and Wrangell Mountains northeast of Cordova in southern Alaska; in fact, they may be found in most of the high mountains of Alaska that are sheltered from the wet coastal storms.

Mountain sheep are hunted for the trophies of the head and

hides. The horns of good specimens have a spread of some twenty inches or more, a base of fourteen inches, and a length of upwards of forty inches. The meat of young, tender sheep is likewise valued as a food delicacy.

Elk, muskox, bison, or western buffalo, and yak have been imported into certain portions of Alaska. There is as yet no open season on these transplanted animals, but when they have multiplied in sufficient numbers, hunting probably will be permitted.

The Alaska Game Commission meets annually to make recommendations to the Fish and Wildlife Service and to the Secretary of the Interior for amendments and changes in the existing game regulations. Therefore, it would be wise for the prospective hunter to procure a copy of the current regulations from the Fish and Wildlife Service in Juneau at the time he prepares for his hunt. (See Appendix for an outline of game laws and bag limits.)

Game birds, including several species of grouse and ptarmigan, as well as migratory wild fowl, have furnished through the years a valuable food supply throughout Alaska for both natives and whites. Some game birds, like animals of Alaska, undergo cycles of marked increase and decrease in numbers. They increase to great abundance every eight to ten years, and then are stricken almost to the vanishing point by epizootic diseases.

In addition to such well-known species of grouse as the ruffed and sharp-tailed and the less familiar spruce and sooty grouse, Alaska has three varieties that turn white in winter. These white grouse, or ptarmigan, are held in high regard by the old-time residents, because they are found throughout the year in the Territory.

During the cycles when their population is growing, the

willow ptarmigan, probably the most numerous of upland game birds, increases to such an extent in certain sections of the Territory that great flocks of from ten to twenty thousand —flocks so large that they obscure the sun when they take to the air with a thunderous roar—have been noted.

Some of these fine game birds, especially the spruce hen (sometimes called fool hen), are so unaccustomed to man that they may be approached almost to within arm's length, and many times, instead of flying, will walk away, clucking and ruffling their feathers not unlike a barnyard hen. It is a sore temptation to shoot them when they stand quietly beside the road within a few feet of a car, and few people are able to resist knocking over half a dozen from the car window, as they are a delicious and tender table delicacy. The law provides that they may not be shot within thirty-three feet of the center of any road. (See Appendix for regulations and bag limits covering game birds and migratory wild fowl.)

The most common varieties of ducks in Alaska are the pintail, mallard, American widgeon, green-winged teal, and greater and lesser scaups. Other varieties are ringnecks, shovelers, gadwalls, blue-winged teals, and canvasbacks. The American and Barrow's goldeneyes also are abundant along the coast line, and the bufflehead and harlequin are nearly as plentiful.

Four species of the beautiful eider ducks nest along the Arctic and Bering coasts. Ducks from other hemispheres sometimes reach Alaska, including the European teal, which nests in Alaska, the European widgeon, the Baikal and falcated teals, the pochard, and the European goldeneye; these last-named five species occur only occasionally in parts of the Territory.

Many species of wild geese are found in Alaska, and eight kinds nest there. The most common are three types of the Canadian goose. Two varieties of white geese, both with jet-black wing tips, visit Alaska; also the lesser snow goose and the tiny Ross's goose, the nest of which has only recently been found, for the first time, in the Perry River district, Northwest Territory, Canada.

The speckle-bellied goose, said to have been the progenitor of the domestic goose, is a common nester in Alaska. Here, too, is found the magnificent Emperor goose, which seldom leaves Alaska and the Aleutians. These geese, especially the males, have beautiful plumage and distinctive markings. Their color is blue, intermingled with black, white, and gray. Their feet and legs are bright orange; the upper part of the neck is snow-white; and the bill resembles delicate translucent mother-of-pearl.

Great flocks of black brant have their nesting grounds along the western and northern shores of Alaska.

Most Alaska migratory wild fowl, as elsewhere, head southward with the first cold snap in the fall and return with the first warm winds as harbingers of spring.

There are certain areas throughout Alaska, described in the Appendix, which have a continuous closed season on all species of animals and birds except wolves and coyotes, and other areas which have continuous closed seasons on certain game and fur animals. The hunter should familiarize himself with these restricted areas in the district where he intends to hunt.

The following section that does not occur in similar regulations in the States is in the Alaska game regulations:

Section 3.—*Taking Animals, Birds, and Game Fishes In Emergencies.*

An Indian or Eskimo, or an explorer, prospector, or traveler, may take animals, birds (except migratory birds), or game fishes in any part of the Territory at any time for food when in need thereof and other sufficient food is not available, but he shall not transport or sell any animal, bird, game fish, or part thereof so taken; and an Indian or Eskimo also may take, possess, and transport, at any time, auks, auklets, guillemots, murres, and puffins and their eggs for food, and their skins for clothing, for his own use and that of his immediate family.

(See Appendix for information concerning hunting, trapping, and game-fishing licenses.)

For hunting big-game animals in Alaska, or for hunting or photographing brown or grizzly bears, a nonresident must be accompanied by a registered guide. The purpose of this regulation is to protect the game, as well as the hunter, and the guide's importance to the hunter is threefold. First: The large bears of Alaska are very dangerous when crowded or wounded, and it is well for any nonresident hunter, unfamiliar with such game, to have an experienced, steady hand and eye and a hard-shooting gun backing him up when he goes out after the big fellows. This backing is especially welcome if the hunter is crossing a treeless tidal flat with no game in sight, and happens to disturb a big brownie from a nap in a wallow. In such a situation he is likely to approach to within a few feet of the bear before either is aware of the other's presence, and thus crowded, the big fellow will often charge—a raging, death-dealing demon of destruction! Here, fast and accurate shooting is required to insure safety from a bad mauling, if not from actual death.

Second: The guide will provide camping equipment, food, and everything else required for the trip except the personal wearing apparel of the hunter, his guns, ammunition, and license. He is an experienced woodsman, acquainted with his territory; he knows the hazards of the trail in any season, and he is an expert in the preparation and shipping of trophies and game.

Third: He protects the hunter from the hazards of becoming lost. And no one that has not had the experience of penetrating Alaska wilds can possibly imagine the actuality of this very real hazard, with the fallen timber in the forested regions overgrown with a wild and almost impenetrable profusion of underbrush, and crisscrossed with perpendicular mountain cliffs and sheer drop-offs practically uncrossable. Not only does the ever present danger of becoming hopelessly lost beset the unaccompanied hunter that is not familiar with the Territory (and they don't always find a lost man in Alaska), but without a guide he usually will lose so much time wandering around trying to get somewhere that he will find little time to hunt. The guide knows the trails, open glades, watercourses, and other means of reaching a given location, and more important than that, he knows where the game may usually be found in the most accessible localities.

The Alaska guide is a high-class outdoor man, very proficient in his work and a thoroughly dependable, enjoyable companion. Treat him as such and the Alaska hunting trip will be as successful as he can make it. It might surprise some outsiders to know that among Alaska's guides are authors of published books, prominent professional men, and businessmen. (See Appendix for names and addresses of Alaska guides and guide district for which each is licensed.)

After a careful study of the guide list, a hunter should select the game animal, or animals, he wishes to hunt, and write—preferably by air mail—two or more guides licensed for the district or districts where the selected game is available. This first contact should be made several months before the expected hunt to assure the availability of a guide at the time the hunter expects to hunt, and so that the guide may have sufficient time in which to make the necessary preparations.

The hunter should by all means inform his guide frankly as to his age, physical condition, hunting ability, and the game he wishes to hunt.

For a successful hunt he should allow at least two weeks, preferably longer, beginning when he arrives at the rendezvous previously arranged with his guide. Inclement weather or other unavoidable delays may take up several days, and he should have not less than ten days of actual hunting time.

The expenses of the hunt, including guide service, food, equipment, and transportation, are of course dependent upon the distance covered and the duration. The guide can give an estimate of the cost if he is informed on the above points. A safe estimate of an average hunt, including all costs, is fifty to one hundred dollars per day per person. And this should procure for the hunter some fine trophies for his collection, as well as some reminiscences that will last the rest of his life.

In Alaska, as elsewhere, better hunting is to be found in isolated, hardly accessible regions. The fine thing about Alaska, from a sportsman's point of view, is that there are so many such regions that the locale is practically the hunter's choice.

Guns are a vital consideration in this big-game area. A great many hunters in the States that have always sworn by a .30-30 as a game getter extraordinary, suitable for anything from a mouse to an elephant, will have to change to a heavier rifle if they wish to be successful in hunting Alaska's biggest game— huge brown and grizzly bears and moose. Conclusive evidence has been produced that .30-30 rifle slugs, and other bullets of the same penetrating power, have glanced off the skulls of Alaska brown bears upon striking at an angle. Neither do they have sufficient shocking power for these monsters.

Winchester is quoted as follows:

> The Model 70 rifle, .30 Govt. '06, .303 and .375 H&H Magnum, and also the 71 rifle and .348 calibre are what we recommend for the game you have specified. The .30 Army Model 95 Winchester rifle that we manufactured at one time can also be used effectively on this type of game, and we suggest that you use the cartridge loaded with the 220-grain bullet.

Remington recommends the Model 270 for Alaska's big game. The .30-'06 Springfield with 220-grain bullet is also satisfactory.

Savage is quoted as follows: "We especially recommend to you the Model 99-EG .300 caliber rifle with 180-grain bullet cartridges for all Alaska big game hunting."

Clothing will depend upon when and where the hunter wishes to hunt. For the extreme cold of the interior and Arctic regions in late fall or winter, ordinary wool clothes topped by a fur or woolen parka, its hood trimmed with wolverine or wolf fur, are desirable. The clothes should not be heavy enough to cause perspiring, as it is dangerous in extremely cold weather.

A complete change of clothing should be available at all times, so that a quick change can be made if perspiring is unavoidable, or when clothes become damp from other causes. Leather boots, known in the States as Maine hunting boots, are suitable. Two pairs of light wool socks are better than one heavy pair.

Proper garments for Alaska trails can be procured almost

anywhere in Alaska, and it is advisable to purchase additions to the ordinary hunting wardrobe after the hunter arrives in Alaska.

Proper sleeping facilities—heavy sleeping bags for extreme temperatures, lighter bags for ordinary use—can usually be obtained for the hunter by his guide. Sleeping bags are valuable not only when it is necessary to camp out, but also when camping in one of the isolated cabins where a permanent camp usually is established. The rough bunks with which most such cabins are equipped need the padding of a sleeping bag; but it is a safe bet that the hunter will not worry much about the softness of his bed after a ten- or twenty-mile tramp into the surrounding country.

No hunter, of course, wants to return empty-handed from an extended hunting trip—and it is unusual for anyone that is a fair shot and has had any previous experience to return from such a trip in Alaska without game. But hunting, like fishing and other outdoor sports, is not altogether a killing game. The magnificent works of nature all about him, unspoiled by the hand of man, add tremendously to the hunter's enjoyment.

Anyone must respond to the splendid panorama unfolded before him as he tops a seven-thousand-foot peak and beholds the blue expanse of the mighty Pacific, or one of its estuaries, studded with emerald-green islands silhouetted on the depths below as though mother nature aspired to give the onlooker a double portion of her grandeur.

The hunter will enjoy the unrestricted freedom spiced with the danger of the trail in this world apart, as he beholds a huge glacier stretching away into the distance, exposing here and there jagged edges of azure-blue outcroppings of that tremendous inner force that grinds down mountains and deposits the grist of its giant mill on the flats below, that forests may gain a foothold.

If the hunter is a true lover of the out-of-doors, his memory of the wild things he saw in their natural habitat—the things he did not kill but left free to go their ways—will far outlive his thrill in the actual killing of game. If he is fortunate he may come upon some unusual sights. Perhaps, after following sounds not unlike those of a steam shovel at work, he may see a huge brown bear weighing more than half a ton, industriously excavating the earth and rock in hot pursuit of a six-inch ground squirrel, which he seldom catches.

Or he may be treated to the ludicrous sight of a black bear attempting to reach down from an overhanging tree and catch a toothsome salmon as it swims below him—an effort that almost always ends with the bear losing his balance and pitching into the cold water. Bruin doesn't particularly like the cold water, but once in, he fishes industriously. Contrary to popular opinion, he seldom knocks the fish out onto the bank with a sweep of his capable paw, but chases them into shallow water where he can grab them in his strong teeth.

One of the most reassuring things about Alaska's wild life is that plans are in operation to perpetuate for us and for posterity the hunting, fishing, and other recreational advantages of this last great frontier. Alaska game laws, although allowing bag limits large enough to satisfy anyone except a confirmed game hog, are devised with consideration of supply, so that there need never be a shortage.

These game laws, easily amended from year to year to take care of unanticipated inroads of disease or depletion from other extraordinary causes, will avoid the disastrous mistakes made in the States fifty or a hundred years ago, when the game supply appeared to be inexhaustible and where promiscuous slaughter has necessitated stringent protective laws and restocking programs. It is within the memory of many elderly people in the States that wild turkeys were hunted for only the choice meat of the breast, and deer were killed for their hams and saddles, the remainder left to rot in the woods.

There are, however, certain disturbing factors in the Alaska game situation, factors that are affecting the future scarcity or abundance of Alaska wild life: Now that roads are being built throughout Alaska, the usual trigger-happy car or truck driver may pop away from his automobile and kill or badly wound big game and other animals. It is not unusual for moose, caribou, or sheep to be shot at, and occasionally hit, by men shooting from automobiles that do not stop to see whether they have killed their illegally shot game or have only wounded it, leaving it to wander off to suffer or die a lingering death. The habit of carrying small pistols or other light firearms in Alaska when traveling over the highways is common practice, especially by residents, and they are all too prone to use them when they encounter game along the highways.

Many of these highway victims are females, protected by law at all seasons, and upon which the future abundance of Alaska's wild life depends.

The productivity of some species is well illustrated by the record of a cow moose, raised as a pet by two prospectors, that produced twenty-three calves in her lifetime of nineteen years. Suppose a careless shot had ended her life at an early age.

A buffalo recently found dead near the highway, and dissected by the Fish and Wildlife Service, had been shot, at various times, by nearly every caliber of pistol and rifle known. And these huge animals have been imported into

Alaska and are rigidly protected by law at all seasons in the hope that they will increase sufficiently to permit hunting them.

On account of the tiny appropriations doled out by Congress, it is impossible to give adequate protection to game in Alaska, and there are not enough wild-life agents to patrol the highways adequately. They have to cover such a large and inaccessible area that wanton violations are common and the violators seldom caught, despite the herculean efforts of these too few men with their few available patrol planes, cars, and boats.

Congress should immediately, before irreparable damage is done, increase the present number of wild-life agents, planes, automobiles, and boats, and the funds to keep them operating throughout the year. The expenditure would be incalculably small compared to the future economic benefit to the Territory.

Thoughtful sportsmen from everywhere will, when hunting in the Territory, adhere rigidly to bag limits and other protective regulations, and help conserve the supply of Alaska wild life for their sons and grandsons. For they, too, if they do not actually come to make their homes in this big, new country, will want the pleasure of visiting this unspoiled wilderness where there is wild life in abundance.

> *Do you honestly, earnestly think now and then*
> *Of leaving the youngsters their part?*
> *If you don't, I'm afraid, friend, you're that other kind,*
> *And haven't a sportsman's heart.*

CHAPTER THREE

Fishing

IT is almost impossible to exaggerate the size or numbers of fish that may be caught in any one of the hundreds of streams and lakes with which Alaska abounds. Nor is it necessary to make long, costly trips to take unbelievably fine catches of steelhead, cutthroat, Dolly Varden, rainbow, grayling, and, in some localities stocked in recent years, eastern brook trout. Dozens of inland lakes are literally alive with scrappy northern pike; other lakes yield native species of trout weighing up to sixty pounds.

Along Alaska's shore line, salmon, halibut, and other salt-water fish are found in great numbers. The southern and southeastern coasts especially teem with schools of mighty king salmon, which have been known to reach a weight of 125 pounds, and the smaller but fighting coho. Here also are deep-sea bass that tax the heavy-duty tackle, and halibut that can be taken in any desired quantity. Fishing from the docks of nearly any town in southeastern Alaska, when the salmon canneries are operating and dumping offal into the water, will produce a fish with nearly every cast. Two hooks on the line will usually catch two fish at a time. If too large a bait for the fish to swallow is used, a dozen or more will follow it to the surface if it is retrieved slowly. Newcomers never cease to marvel that fish so large—sixteen to twenty-four inches long—may be taken as fast as small perch are taken in lakes and streams in the States. They are good eating fish, too, if soaked for a time before cooking to eliminate some of the oil. Codfish predominate, although flounder and sole are also common. Some Alaskans salt them down in the manner of salt mackerel.

A setting of indescribable grandeur adds zest to the sport of fresh-water fishing in Alaska. On right and left rise majestic mountains; crystal-clear streams swish by one's feet; lakes glitter like broad mirrors in the sun. A deer, moose, or bear makes a hasty retreat as the angler approaches, and a beaver slaps the water with its broad tail to warn its fellows of possible danger. A wild duck with her brood swims quickly and silently away. A land otter surfaces and looks inquiringly at the intruder. An eagle screams its defiance as it catapults itself from the branches of a tall spruce or cottonwood.

Many lakes and streams in inaccessible parts of Alaska have yet to be fished for the first time by a white man.

Generally speaking, steelhead, cutthroat, and Dolly Varden trout are common to streams and lakes near the coast line; rainbow, eastern brook, and grayling farther inland.

The various species of trout are taken here on the same tackle and in much the same manner as in the States. A five- to eight-ounce fly rod or light casting rod of bamboo or steel is desirable, with the steel rod holding preference because of durability. An extra fly rod and several extra tips are absolutely necessary if the fisherman is to have uninterrupted fishing, as the tackle busters encountered throughout Alaska wreak havoc with rods. A fisherman never knows, when he drops his fly or plug into a stream, just what may strike next; and likely as not one or more ten- to twenty-pound salmon will smash into his light tackle before his fishing trip is over, and something has to break. Unless the fisherman has had previous experience with large rainbows, he will encounter the most stubborn bull-like rushes, double flips, and tail walking he has ever tried to stop with a fly rod; and the chances are good that he won't stop all of them without a broken rod. In tackling these giant rainbows—some of them twenty to thirty inches long—more than one fisherman has come back from a fishing trip with only the handle and first section of his rod intact.

Late spring, summer, and early fall are the best times to fish in Alaska, although the season in most of the Territory is not defined by statute. Inclement weather usually restricts fishing in other months, also lack of runs, although early trout runs have been observed in southeastern Alaska in the latter part of February or early March, and good catches are made up to the first of November. In the streams and lakes of the interior and far north, grayling and rainbow fishing continues into early October, and lake trout also are taken in favorable weather into early autumn, but these last-named streams and lakes are not clear of ice and available for fishing until June.

Bait fishermen, using salmon eggs with or without spinners, take record catches of all species of trout. Fly-fishermen can get a limit of trout almost any time during the summer using the old reliable black gnat, coachman, royal coachman, Lord Baltimore, or any one of a dozen other well-known flies, or very small trout flies. In some lakes and streams in this fisherman's paradise the fish will take nearly any lure offered—plugs, spinners, and spoons take limit catches. Light fly-rod spoons are very effective, and a red-and-white striped casting spoon is especially good in early fall. (See Appendix for creel limits, licenses, and seasons.)

An example of the fishing to be had in well-fished water

near the most densely populated section of Alaska is revealed in a letter from Juneau, a portion of which is quoted as follows: "It was my pleasure, not long ago, to visit Turner Lake near Juneau, arriving there late one afternoon, spending all the next day fishing, and returning home on the third day.... In that time we brought away sixty cutthroat trout ranging up to eighteen inches."

In the same area, Auke Lake on the highway a few miles from Juneau produces many fine catches in season. A fisherman recently landed a nice string of Dolly Varden and cutthroat trout at the outlet of the lake, and ended up with his fly rod badly sprung by a large salmon that broke his fly line; then had the pawl and worm pulled out of his casting reel by a fifteen-pound salmon, which he finally landed.

Another favorite fishing place near by is the power dam on Salmon Creek, accessible by a footpath that leaves the Glacier Highway some two and a half miles from Juneau. The reservoir above the dam and the stream below offer excellent fishing for Colorado brook trout, imported into the area.

Peterson Lake near Juneau produces some good catches of Dolly Varden trout of small size, and fine steelhead fishing is enjoyed in Peterson Creek up to the falls during April and early May.

Also in the Juneau area, accessible by trail from the Glacier Highway, is Montana Creek and Windfall Lake, well supplied with Dolly Varden and cutthroat trout.

Admiralty Creek, twenty miles from Juneau and available by boat, offers fine steelhead fishing, and four and a half miles farther by trail is Youngs Lake, well stocked with cutthroat. There is a boat and shelter cabin at Youngs Lake.

Bear Creek in the same area is reached by boat and trail and offers excellent cutthroat fishing.

Rhinestone and Grindstone creeks, about ten miles from Juneau by boat, are fine trout streams. Carlson Creek, Annex Creek, and Taku River a little farther along are also excellent trout streams. Taku Harbor and Limestone Inlet are outlets for several good trout streams, and the Berners Bay Area on Lynn Canal is the outlet for several other good cutthroat trout streams.

Lake Florence, about forty miles by air from Juneau, available also by boat and trail, is wonderful fishing water.

And these are only a few of the many good fishing streams and lakes in the immediate vicinity of Juneau, the capital city.

Visitors to Ketchikan will find Ketchikan Creek flowing through the heart of the city. Salmon in great numbers may be seen during July, August, and September, attempting to climb the falls directly below the Bawden Street bridge. Steelhead trout may be caught along the creek in the early spring and summer, and Dolly Varden, cutthroat, and rainbow are also native to this stream.

Near-by Ward Creek Valley, available by car over a spur road from the highway, has four nice lakes well stocked with Dolly Varden and cutthroat, and one lake has eastern brook trout that have been transplanted there.

One of the best trout streams in the Ketchikan area empties into Thorne Bay and is available by mail boat. Karta River, likewise reached by mail boat, is an excellent steelhead, rainbow, and cutthroat stream. Cabin Creek on Skowl Arm and Kegan Creek on Moira Sound are fine steelhead and rainbow streams, reached by special boat.

The Rudyard Bay area near Ketchikan, one of the most picturesque spots in the district, has several excellent lakes and streams alive with rainbow and Dolly Varden, and near-by Nooya Lake is noted for its large landlocked Dolly

Vardens. The Long Lake and Reflection Lake areas, reached by mail boat, are noted for cutthroat and steelhead fishing. The Bailey Bay–Bell Island areas have excellent fishing streams and lakes. Both are on the mail-boat route out of Ketchikan. Bell Island has a number of modern cabins, with hot baths from the near-by springs. Bailey Bay likewise has hot springs, and a shelter cabin and skiffs for the convenience of fishermen.

Yes Bay, forty miles northwest of Ketchikan, has excellent rainbow fishing in the creek that empties into the bay. Accommodations for visitors are available, and transportation is by mail boat from Ketchikan.

And these fishing places near Ketchikan, named for the guidance of visitors to that district, represent only a very small proportion of the near-by fishing spots.

There are two good fishing lakes on the Milton Lake trail a few miles from Cordova. There are also a number of good trout lakes on Canoe Pass Trail. Makaka Point Trail skirts six excellent cutthroat trout lakes. You can get to all of these trails by boat from Cordova. Dolly Varden and rainbow trout fishing is good in the connecting streams.

Summer visitors to Cordova should try the salt-water bays and inlets near by, even the piers fronting the town, as large halibut may be taken with rod and reel.

The largest rainbow trout taken in Alaska, some measuring upwards of thirty inches, come from the Russian River of southern Alaska above Seward. The Alaska Railroad, as well as 125 miles of automobile road, leads from Seward into a fisherman's paradise with such well-known fishing spots, in addition to Russian River, as Ptarmigan Creek, Quartz Creek, Cooper Creek, and adjoining lakes. Roadhouses and meals are available near the fishing grounds. It is doubtful if fishing better than that in the above district can be found anywhere in an accessible region in Alaska. This area can also be reached from Anchorage by train.

Accessible by boat and trail from Sitka are two excellent trout lakes, Green Lake and Salmon Lake in the Silver Bay area. Indian River offers fair fishing and is within walking distance, if you start from the Sheldon Jackson School. Thimbleberry Lake and Heart Lake also are reached by trail from the highway and afford fair trout fishing, which should improve as these lakes have had artificial stocking in recent years.

Many beautiful creeks and lakes are in easy reach along the Richardson and other Alaska highways. Valdez, at the southernmost end of the Richardson Highway, has several good trout streams within a mile of the town.

Near Tonsina Lodge, eighty miles above Valdez where Little Tonsina River empties into Big Tonsina, is excellent grayling fishing. There recently was observed a good illustration of the abundance of fish in Alaska waters: A twelve-year-old lad stood on a rock out in the stream and industriously flipped grayling onto the rocky bank. Each time he caught a fish he jumped from his rock to the bank, whacked the fish over the head with a club, and strung it on a forked stick. Despite all the commotion and noise of landing and killing his catch, and the effort and arm-slinging required to get his line out, he continued to plop fish after fish onto the bank. He was using a steel bait-casting rod for a fly rod, had two very small trout flies tied tandem on a small leader; and he never changed flies. He fished within ten feet of the rock upon which he stood, in water not more than eighteen inches deep and so clear that every pebble on the bottom was visible. He made no effort at concealment, was in almost constant motion, and fish continued to strike, not only his flies but also small insects floating by, and they kept up a constant turmoil in the water all about. And this was within fifty yards of the old highway, within sight and sound of the new highway, and within walking distance of the lodge.

Tonsina Lodge offers modern conveniences, including meals, for the sportsman.

Eleven miles above Tonsina the Chitina Road branches off the Richardson Highway. And near the little town of Chitina, some thirty miles from the above-mentioned road fork, is a chain of several beautiful lakes. The mineral and vegetable content of the water makes it appear dark, and the water has a decided vegetable and mineral taste. These lakes are literally alive with grayling, so crowded that they do not reach normal size and rarely run over ten inches. It is an ideal place to take the family for an outing, as these small grayling can be caught on nearly any kind of bait or with small flies. Two flies on a line will often produce two fish at a cast.

Here, when funds will permit, the Fish and Wildlife Service can develop with a small amount of artificial stocking, some of the finest fishing lakes in Alaska. A few lake trout added to the enormous grayling population should multiply bountifully and tend to thin out the grayling so that they in turn could grow to normal size. And the highway skirts the very edges of the lakes for a mile or more. Accommodations for fishermen are available in near-by Chitina.

Farther along the Richardson Highway, also along the new Glenn Highway, which branches off toward Palmer and Anchorage, are many beautiful trout lakes and streams.

Excellent fishing may be enjoyed near Paxson Lodge which is located on the Richardson Highway about halfway from Valdez to Fairbanks. Two large lakes, Paxson and Summit, are in the immediate vicinity, and the highway skirts them for several miles. These lakes are noted for their huge lake trout which attain a length of several feet and weigh upwards of forty pounds. They bite readily on spoons and other trolled baits, but the larger specimens take live whitefish ten to twelve inches long more readily than any other bait.

These two lakes are connected by a swift-flowing creek that runs parallel to the highway and only a few steps from the lodge. This creek produces some of the largest grayling of any creek in Alaska, the largest specimens measuring over twenty inches, and the average sixteen to eighteen inches.

At the outlet to Summit Lake, and easily reached by boat from Dr. Huffman's boat landing on the highway, is a fast stretch of water absolutely alive with rainbow and grayling.

The water in this narrow channel is often literally churned to foam by huge rainbows in hot pursuit of grayling, and occasionally both grayling and rainbow clear the water during the mad chase. These large fish tax the ability of even an expert fly-fisherman, and it is doubtful if any fly-fisherman can come away from that excellent strip of rainbow water after a day's fishing with a whole fly rod. It is no place for an amateur, as the water is fairly well fished, which makes the fish somewhat wary, and further, an amateur would be extremely lucky to land a fish, even if he did hook it in the fast, mossy, rocky stream, for the fish employ every trick known from lively acrobatics to long bullheaded rushes. However, if large live minnows could be procured and used for bait, and the stream fished with a steel rod and heavy line, there is little doubt that some record fish could be taken.

On up the Richardson Highway near Fairbanks are several good grayling streams and two excellent lakes, Birch Lake and Lake Harding. Accommodations for visitors are available near these lakes.

Along the Steese Highway, beyond Fairbanks, are many good grayling streams easily accessible from the highway.

Recently, far out on the Steese Highway, a little old lady was observed hurrying across the highway, fly rod in one hand and a bucket in the other. Just beyond was a bridge across a gurgling, swift-flowing little stream, and on the other side of the bridge was a neat bungalow. As the season was so late—mid-September—it was somewhat of a surprise to see a fly-fisherman, or fisherwoman, way up there within a hundred miles of the Arctic Circle. The day was nippy but clear, with the sky turquoise—so common in that area. The lady was warmly dressed, and she literally radiated good health and the joy of living in the out-of-doors.

She explained, somewhat apologetically, that fish were supposed to have departed the small streams at that season, then smilingly reached into the bucket and displayed several nice grayling which she had caught above the bridge, and she was on her way downstream for further tries.

Women throughout Alaska are ardent followers of Izaak Walton, and many of them carry their own pack boards and equipment into rugged, inaccessible regions. It is not at all unusual for a woman to hike twelve to fifteen miles in a day, carrying a thirty- or forty-pound pack—a town resident at that!

Good fishing is so general throughout the Territory that it is unfair to direct a sport fisherman to any one part, and only a few of the hundreds of lakes and streams throughout Alaska are mentioned herein. Those mentioned are in the vicinity of some town or highway and are easily accessible by private boat or car, or by public conveyance—mail boat, bus, or railroad. Nearly all are available by plane, especially along the coast. They are specifically singled out for the benefit of visitors to Alaska that have a limited time and wish to try their skill in some near-by stream or lake.

The fisherman will find both salt-water and fresh-water fishing easily accessible from Seward, Anchorage, Cordova, and Valdez in southern Alaska, and from Ketchikan, Wrangell, Petersburg, Juneau, Sitka, Haines, and Skagway in southeastern Alaska. Busses, railroads, or mail boats leave from nearly all of these towns, and arrangements can be made for the fisherman and his equipment to be dropped off near a good fishing lake or stream, with shelter cabin or other accommodation near by. He can catch the return bus, train, or boat at a given date. Float planes are available in most coast towns, where more extensive trips may be arranged into less accessible regions. In Alaska, as elsewhere, more easily caught fish are to be had in the less accessible regions.

Portions of southern and southeastern Alaska are subject to so much rainfall that it is essential that the fisherman have a raincoat with cape, or wear a turndown hat with brim wide enough to keep the rain from going down his collar. He also will need hip boots and extra-heavy wool socks, or two pairs of lighter wool socks, to protect his feet from the cold that penetrates the boots in the cold water. Light wool trousers are also preferable for tucking into the boots.

A light sleeping bag is necessary if the fisherman expects to camp out in the open or in one of the shelter cabins. During late spring and early summer mosquito netting is essential, and in some localities, head nets and gloves are necessary.

A good pack board is needed if the fisherman expects to hike into less accessible regions. And it will pay anyone well, if he is unfamiliar with pack boards, to get advice from an expert on the kind of pack board to buy, and how to pack it.

A bottle or two of preserved salmon eggs is good equipment

for any fisherman's kit. Fish will take eggs when they refuse other lures. Worms catch more eastern brook trout than any other lure.

A feature of salt-water sport fishing is a "salmon derby" held each year in Juneau. Fishermen gather from far and near to compete for prizes strip-fishing for the mighty king salmon. The most popular equipment for this sport of kings is a light salt-water bamboo rod of six ounces or more, with agate, porcelain, or rustproof metal guides, and a salt-water reel with star drag, big enough to hold two hundred yards of thirty-five-pound-test raw silk line. A fifteen-pound-test leader is preferred.

Strip-fishing, the manner of taking king salmon during the derby, is a comparatively new sport. The hook is baited with a strip cut from the side of a herring, and dropped over the side of a stationary or slow-moving boat. Allowed to sink a hundred feet or more, the line is retrieved, or "stripped," with short jerks toward the surface to lure the salmon.

And a great deal of care is observed in cutting and baiting the strip of herring. Unless it is cut and baited in a manner that will impart to the bait a lifelike motion, the catch will be small.

Fishermen in Alaska, as elsewhere the world over, experiment with all types of lures and baits. Spoons or plugs, trolled behind a boat moving at three or four knots, are used by both sport and commercial fishermen. And in this type of fishing some of the most unusual "gang baits" ever devised are to be seen. These unusual baits, consisting of a string of spoons, spinners, and other bright-colored contraptions, are strung out for more than a foot. A casual glance at one of them brings forth the thought that any self-respecting fish would flee from such a monstrosity. But some unknown factor in fish psychology causes the fish to tag along behind the spinning, whirling thingumagig, and the fish finally takes a nip at the lower end of it where the hook is located.

Fishing for king salmon is by no means limited to the Juneau area. The many channels, bays, and inlets near Petersburg and Wrangell are favorite spots, and hundreds of these fish are caught every year with light sporting tackle within a few hundred feet of the wharves of those towns. The bays and inlets near Ketchikan and the channel both below and above the town are excellent king areas. Hundreds of square miles of bay area throughout southeastern Alaska offer splendid opportunities for the king salmon as well as the coho, during the summer months.

There is little danger of Alaska streams being depleted of fish within any reasonable time if present conservation measures are observed by fishermen. However, sufficient funds have not been furnished from Washington to man and equip properly the Alaska Fish and Wildlife Service, and for that reason the few men, planes, boats, and cars cannot possibly cover adequately the thousands of square miles of territory where sport fishing is available. Violations of creel limits are common, and one wild-life agent reports that he counted 120 fine trout on one stringer left lying on a rock beside a stream in southern Alaska, rotting in the sun.

Such game-hog tactics are said to have led to the necessity of a closed season on certain streams, and a lower bag limit than is allowed elsewhere in the Territory.

If Alaska and outside fishermen wish to enjoy in future the present unrestricted seasons and adequate bag limits, they all must zealously observe those limits and insist that others do likewise.

When trout are striking—the day of days—
When they hit anything, everywhere;
Do you find real pleasure in turning some back?
If you don't, is your conscience clear?

CHAPTER FOUR

Travel

ALASKA offers some of the most spectacular creations of nature to be seen anywhere on earth.

Mountains? You can look up and up—five thousand, yes ten thousand feet—then turn and look down into a gorge behind you another five thousand feet! And Alaska's mountains, every foot of them, are blanketed with a riot of color. Flowers—blue, red, yellow, white—every color of the rainbow, find a foothold in clefts and crevices in summer; patches of fireweed cling to the bronze ore-bearing, copper-tinted mountainsides in autumn, and the lower expanses are blue and red with acres of blueberries and low-bush cranberries. Year-round snowbanks add startling contrast. Bring along plenty of color film for your camera—you'll use up reel after reel.

Primeval forests? You can step off any man-made trail in southern and southeastern Alaska, and immediately you find yourself swallowed up in a veritable fairyland that rivals even a Walt Disney production. If you have never been to Alaska it is difficult for you to visualize an Alaska forest in all of its weird, uneasy beauty. It's like stepping into another world. Huge trees—two or three generations of them—have fallen, one across the other, and from the stumps of these century-old monarchs of the forest that now lie prostrate, there has

sprouted yet another generation of trees that tower upward
a hundred feet or more. For fallen trees do not decay quickly
in this cool, damp climate; instead, they are soon covered by
a heavy layer of pale green moss, which preserves them almost
indefinitely. A thick covering of this same moss spreads over
the ground, the rocks—everything; and this covering deadens
the sound of your own footfalls. There is an eerie stillness.

Your feeling of awe at the strangeness—that age-old fear of
dim forests where dangers once lurked—soon wears away, and
then you begin to enjoy this unmarred wilderness. You discover a little spring-fed brook, lined on either side with ferns
interspersed with the broad green leaves of skunk cabbage
and ground dogwood with its bright red berries. Then, on
a near-by cliff, sitting up motionless as a statue, you see a fat
round marmot gazing at you in fascinated interest.

Before you wander far you will come to a trail—a game
trail. It won't register on you at first; but you straighten up
with a start when you realize that the fresh spoor beside the
trail is that of a huge bear, and the near-by rotten tree trunk
was torn to shreds by the claws of a bear in search of grubs.
Your eyes follow the trail, worn smooth by countless feet.
You peer uneasily into the forest on either side—maybe throw
a cautious glance over your shoulder –and then thank almighty
Providence and Alaska law for the heavy six-shooter you are
permitted to carry. Up to now it has been a nuisance, flopping
there in the holster against your leg, but suddenly it feels
downright comforting. Don't use it unless you absolutely
have to, and you seldom, if ever, have to. This little bit of
ever present spicing of danger adds an unbelievable amount
of thrill to Alaska trails.

And whatever you do, if you are alone and new to Alaska's

forests, *don't get lost*. Stay in sight of the forest trail or other landmark.

Yes, Alaska offers an abundance of unexplored wilderness, wild life, fishing, hunting, and other outdoor recreation.

But you will want to plan your trip well in order to avoid most of the inconveniences of a new, unsettled country. There is a lot of enjoyment in planning and anticipation. It's a part of any trip.

Before you leave the States you should choose your route throughout Alaska. Your plans should take into consideration the length of time you can spare for the trip, and how much money you can afford to spend. A trip to southeastern Alaska, nearest to U.S. and Canadian ports, can be completed within a couple of weeks, and the cost is three to five hundred dollars, including transportation to and from Seattle or a near-by British Columbia port. A more extensive trip through the heart of the Territory, requires about thirty-five days to complete and the cost is six hundred to a thousand dollars, depending upon the number of side trips you wish to make, your mode of transportation, etc. (See Appendix for detailed transportation and other costs.)

Usually a journey to and from a destination is somewhat boresome. Not so this Alaska trip. It seems that you are hardly out of Seattle when you begin to see things. Here, above the tree-lined inland passage, you will observe the first snow-capped mountain peaks. Shore birds are everywhere; and if you are fortunate you will get an occasional view of a hair seal and perhaps a whale as it swims slowly away from the oncoming steamer. Here also you see the first icebergs, fore-runners of the huge glaciers so common throughout Alaska. And before you know it, a couple of days have passed and you are in Ketchikan.

Alaska! You can hardly realize that you have arrived. Especially if it is midsummer and you see a whole beach alive with bathers.

Ketchikan is a modern little city, with a long water front, and with hundreds of small craft of all descriptions anchored in the bay. Modern hotels, good restaurants, supermarkets, curio shops, up-to-date dry-goods stores and other city-like accommodations are to be found in Ketchikan. And you will want to visit one or more of the many large canneries and perhaps a lumber mill while there. Be sure to visit the Fishery Products Laboratory. There, in addition to an explanation of the latest methods of processing fish, you will find an interesting exhibit of many specimens of fish and shellfish common to Alaska waters, including octopus, wolf eel, sea cucumber, lobsters, and the giant king crab with a leg spread of several feet.

Ketchikan is the home of the *Alaska Sportsman*, for twelve years Alaska's outstanding magazine. A well-stocked bookstore, specializing in Alaska books, and a curio shop and museum are maintained at the *Sportsman's* headquarters. Visitors are heartily welcomed by the genial editor, Mr. Emery F. Tobin, and his pleasant staff.

Ketchikan Creek with its cascading falls flows through the heart of the city. Near by is a beautiful little park, and just beyond is the beginning of a footpath to the ski cabin and to the summit of Deer Mountain, from which vantage point you will have a fine view of the harbor and boat traffic. On very clear days you sometimes can see as far as the British Columbia coast nearly a hundred miles away. This mountain usually retains patches of snow throughout the summer.

The largest concentration of totem poles on the continent

is in the Tlingit Indian village three miles south of Ketchikan, reached by automobile, taxi, or bus.

A good road leads seventeen miles north from Ketchikan. Near-by Ward Creek Valley has four beautiful lakes, with well-marked trails for hiking. Watch for deer during spring, summer, and autumn, and keep a sharp lookout for bears. Here also you may see beavers busily at work.

Don't fail to take a trip to the Loring area, often visited by mail boats and by special boats. Inquire at the office of the *Alaska Sportsman* for information on sailings.

A footpath leads from where the Loring boat docks, skirting a chain of beautiful lakes, to Naha Falls. This two-and-a-half-mile trail will give you an almost perfect picture of primeval Alaska wilderness, including the bear trails and bear sign.

At the falls you will find a shelter and observation shed provided by the Forest Service, where bears appear in late summer and early fall as they come out of the dense timber and go into the water below the falls to catch salmon. Watch especially for the bear with the broken jaw. He has been coming to the falls almost daily for years, and despite his handicap is able to catch a toothsome salmon for his dinner. Most of the bears at Naha Falls are black bears, and you are permitted to photograph them without a guide.

A boat trip out of Ketchikan, along the Behm Canal, is a scenic trip of much interest. Here are wooded islands and bays and inlets with level, flower-studded beaches where you may beach your boat and explore the easily accessible valleys. Other bays along the canal have precipitous walls rising almost perpendicular for hundreds of feet from the water's edge.

From Ketchikan your boat follows the beautiful inland passage to Wrangell, a lumbering and fishing town rich in history and romance of the gold-rush days. Here prospectors were outfitted as they headed up the Stikine River toward the Yukon by way of the Teslin Trail. Wrangell, at an early date, was headquarters of the then powerful and warlike Stikine Indians.

You then continue along the inland passage toward Petersburg. Near-by Le Conte Glacier, said to be the most southernly tidewater glacier on the Pacific Coast, hurls many gigantic icebergs into the water of Frederick Sound. Wrangell Narrows brings everyone on deck, as the ship glides through such a narrow channel that it seems almost to touch the forested walls.

For a mile or more before you reach Petersburg the attractive homes of many of its citizens dot the drive along the shore. Petersburg, with its fishing industries and near-by fur farms, is claimed by some to be the wealthiest town per capita in Alaska. From this little city there is an unsurpassed view of the snow, ice, and pinnacles of the near-by mountain range, culminating in a spire of rock rising 1,600 feet above the mountain range to a height of 9,000 feet. This steeple of rock is called the Devil's Thumb and has been referred to as "horribly magnificent" and "uncommonly awful" by an early visitor to the region.

Baird Glacier north of Petersburg is the most southernly known nesting grounds of the arctic tern, and they may be observed there by the thousands during the nesting season.

Don't miss a trip to near-by Anan Creek. Here, in a bear refuge, many black bears congregate during the salmon runs, and stockaded observation points afford ample opportunity for photographing the bears in their natural surroundings. Brown bears may also be seen here occasionally.

Next is Juneau, the capital city of Alaska. Visit by all means the Territorial Museum and Historical Library. The many exhibits there, and the information you will obtain about Alaska, both past and present, will materially enhance your knowledge of the Territory and make more pleasurable the rest of your trip. There you may see exhibits of Indian and Eskimo handiwork, early historical exhibits, flora and fauna of Alaska, and other interesting displays too numerous to mention. In the animal-pelt exhibit may be seen the luxurious pelt of the sea otter, much sought by the early Russians for the imperial household. And there also is a library, filled to capacity with valuable collections of books about Alaska.

A few miles north of Juneau is Mendenhall Glacier and Auke Lake. Mendenhall, one of the most visited glaciers in Alaska, is unique in that you may walk up to the very face of the tremendous ice mountain, or skirt around the edge and walk along the top of it. Everybody who visits Alaska comes away with pictures of the glacier and lake, one of the most beautiful and most photographed spots in all Alaska. Cutthroat and Dolly Varden trout lurk in the lake and in the little stream at the outlet of the lake, and you should try your luck with a fly.

Auke Bay, Auke Village recreation area, Port Louisa, and Port Lena are a short distance farther along the highway, and you will be amazed at the many attractive summer homes along the bay and will enjoy the bay-view scenery along the route. A bus line from Juneau serves this entire area.

Seventy-six miles by boat, twenty-six miles by air, from Juneau is the famous Pack Creek, where an observation platform has been erected by the Forest Service for viewing and photographing brown bears fishing for salmon. This platform is in a tree and is reached by a steel ladder. The bears regularly pulled down the original wood ladder. It is the only place in all Alaska where you may safely observe these huge beasts in their natural surroundings.

You will also wish to visit the famous Alaska-Juneau gold mine, a landmark at the edge of the city of Juneau, which has been one of the largest producers of gold for the nation.

Just across the busy canal, spanned by an automobile bridge, is the town of Douglas. Several miles of scenic highway wind around the foot of the mountains on the Douglas side of the canal, and many attractive suburban homes are located there.

Skagway, your next stop, is located at the head of the Lynn Canal and produces some of the most beautiful flowers and boasts some of the finest vegetable gardens in Alaska. Skagway was the outfitting point for many early-day prospectors, and was the onetime headquarters of the famous (or infamous) "Soapy" Smith. It is the southern terminus of the White Pass and Yukon Railroad, ending in Whitehorse, Yukon Territory. Don't fail to make the trip to Whitehorse over this sturdy little narrow-gauge line which did such yeoman's service during the war. Along its route is some of the most beautiful, breath-taking scenery to be found anywhere.

Haines, adjoining the famous Chilkoot Barracks, which was until 1940 the only U.S. Army post in the Territory, is situated near the upper end of the main body of Lynn Canal. Not far from Haines is a fine agricultural area, especially productive of strawberries, vegetables, and root crops.

Over on the gulf side of Baranof Island is the historical town of Sitka, reached by passenger boat. Sitka, former capital of Russian America, is in an area of magnificent scenery and has several ancient buildings of historical interest, including the famous old Russian church with its icons, paintings, and jewels. At one time Sitka boasted what was said to be the only castle ever built on the North American continent—Baranof

Castle—but it was destroyed by fire. In the early days there was a foundry in Sitka, and Russians cast bells there. Some of these bells found their way into the old California missions.

Your travels throughout Alaska will next take you across a portion of the Gulf of Alaska, sometimes as peaceful as a baby's dream but often beset by heavy swells and huge waves that only an old sea dog can enjoy. Along the shore of the gulf, you pass the world's highest coastal mountain range, with such tremendous, frost-capped giants as Mt. Crillon, Mt. Fairweather, Mt. Vancouver, Mt. Cook, and Mt. St. Elias towering from twelve to eighteen thousand feet above the level of the sea. Numerous huge glaciers come into view including the great Malaspina, said to be the largest coastal glacier in the world, with an area of some 1,500 square miles.

Your boat touches at Cordova, beautiful little mountain-edge town on the southern coast, situated in one of the most scenic parts of Alaska and especially noted for its magnificent forests and island-dotted seacoast.

Here is the home of Dr. Will H. Chase, mayor of Cordova for more than thirty years, scientist, author, and guide for numerous expeditions for specimens of wild life for the Museum of Natural History in New York, and one of the few sources in the world through which a live wolverine may be obtained. His private museum contains specimens of minerals, metals, bones of prehistoric animals, skins, mountings, and some of the finest totems in the world. His interesting book *The Sourdough Pot* is a vivid account of the experience of two old-timers during the gold-rush era, and substantiates a great deal of Alaska lore. He now has two later books—*The Alaska Big Brown Bear*, and *Reminiscences of Captain Billy Moore*—published by Burton Publishing Company, Kansas City.

Valdez, a short distance up the coast, is a picturesque town built on the terminal moraine of a receding glacier, and is the southern terminus of the Richardson Highway to interior Alaska.

Out of Valdez, steamers sometimes pull up to the face of Columbia Glacier, said to be the largest glacier in the world approachable by ocean steamers. When the steamship whistle blows, this huge ice cliff occasionally releases great masses of ice, which tumble into the sea with a roar that reverberates from mountain peak to mountain peak, and send a wave large enough to sink a small ship tumbling toward the steamer.

Seward, still farther up the coast, is the coastal end of the Alaska Railroad. Here you may continue by steamer or plane southwest to Kodiak Island and the town of Kodiak, said to be the oldest settlement in Alaska. John Burroughs' eulogy of Kodiak is most fitting:

> So secluded, so remote, so peaceful, such a mingling of the domestic, the pastoral, the sylvan with the wild and the rugged; such emerald heights, such flowery vales; such blue arms and recesses of the sea, and such vast green solitude stretching away to the West and to the North and to the South—bewitching Kodiak!

Across the strait from Kodiak in the Katmai National Monument, approachable only by a long and arduous hike requiring several days to complete, is the famous and awe-inspiring Valley of Ten Thousand Smokes. This gigantic outcropping of nature's inner fire is said to have been formed when Katmai Volcano erupted in 1912. The unusual and magnificently fearful place holds even those inured to extraordinary sights spellbound. Thousands of fumaroles issue smoke and steam. A cloud of vapor hangs over the valley and creeps up the slopes. All vegetation was buried under volcanic ash in 1912, and small animals which were unable to flee from the catastrophe were killed. Of late, however, the number of fumaroles is rapidly decreasing, and vegetation is returning to the valley. It is therefore altogether possible that within another decade this interesting sight may withdraw into the bowels of the earth whence it came.

Upon your return to Seward, you may enter by railroad or bus a scenic hunter's and fisherman's paradise equaled by few spots on the globe. Good automobile roads traverse the area and trips are easily arranged.

Large bands of mountain sheep are often visible on the slopes east of the Seward Highway between Bear Lake and Moose Pass. Near milepost 21 on the highway, and at the end of the Bear Creek road, are good vantage points for observing sheep.

Many convenient trails have been constructed by the Forest Service from the highway into this game paradise and never-to-be-forgotten scenic wonderland. Fishing streams and lakes abound, and bears, moose, and other Alaska animals are to be found in great numbers throughout the area.

Less than a hundred miles north of Seward on the Alaska Railroad is Anchorage, fastest growing city of Alaska, a beehive of industry and crowded with newcomers. It is a tremendous air terminus, and at its municipal airport 11,500 flights were recently recorded during one month.

A trip of great interest, and one you will not want to miss, is available from Anchorage by car, bus, or rail to the famous Matanuska Valley. Here, you will recall, some two hundred families from the dust-bowl areas were rehabilitated in a group resettlement program (fully described in a later chapter, "Homesteading, Farming, and Ranching"), and here you may see prosperous farms producing marvelous crops of grain, vegetables, berries, poultry, and livestock. These farms lie along the fertile Matanuska River Valley, a scenic area surrounded by high, snow-capped mountains, traversed by many glacial and mountain streams and studded with lakes.

A few miles south of Palmer—the principal town in the valley—and alongside the highway is the source of a clear, spring-fed creek where salmon by the hundreds congregate in late summer and fall to spawn. Spectators often line the highway to watch these fish in the clear shallow water. The fish, apparently oblivious of the onlookers, perform for the grandstand, as they fight and splash about seeking favorable spots in which to spawn.

Even in this open and unshaded place you will find them exceedingly difficult to photograph clearly, and your ingenuity will be taxed to the utmost to get a good picture, despite the fact that they are perfectly exposed to the naked eye in their vivid red spawning coloration.

North by rail from Anchorage is a country of splendid mountain scenery. Your next stop will be Curry, where lunch is served at the Curry Hotel; the train does not carry a diner. (A black bear raided the hotel kitchen recently and had to be shot for its pestiferousness.)

Then you enter Mt. McKinley National Park. Here you should plan for a stopover of several days, as many miles of automobile roads traverse interesting portions of the park and offer easy access to an unexcelled scenic paradise. Cars are available during the summer for side trips throughout the parks, and hiking trails lead in all directions. Good hotel accommodations likewise are available.

A feature of Mt. McKinley Park is towering Mt. McKinley, the highest mountain in North America, reaching upward

20,300 feet toward the sky. Also of special interest is the animal life within the park. Here you will find caribou, with their enormous antlers, in herds of a thousand or more. Moose, mountain sheep, brown and grizzly bears, and various other species of Alaska's abundant wild life may be seen along the roads and trails, also countless smaller animals and many species of birds. Hunting is prohibited in the park, but good fishing is available in the many lakes and streams.

Fairbanks, fittingly known as the "Golden Heart" of Alaska because of the tremendous near-by gold production, will be your next stop. Fairbanks is near the center of the Territory and is a transportation hub with railroad, bus, and air routes going forth in all directions. Near by is the University of Alaska, the only school of higher learning in the Territory. It is a fully accredited college with entrance requirements comparable to those in the States, and nearly 25 per cent of its students are from the States. The Agricultural Experiment Station is located close by, and the University also has an excellent museum, containing among other interesting items many exhibits of the bones and tusks of the mammoth, as well as remains of other prehistoric animals, and exhibits of art work of early inhabitants of Alaska. Here also is a sea-otter pelt, an item to be found in only a few museums in the world; and among other mounted specimens of Alaska animals is an albino moose.

The University buildings are located on a promontory overlooking the beautiful farming area of the Tanana Valley, where fine crops of grain and produce are grown.

From Fairbanks you may cut back to Nenana and transfer to a steamship, and for the next several days cruise leisurely down the Tanana, stopping at the town of Tanana, turning up the Yukon to Rampart—Rex Beach's frontier home—then to

Fort Yukon (you cross the Arctic Circle just before you reach Fort Yukon), Circle City, and Eagle.

Next you arrive at Dawson, Yukon Territory, well-known town of the Klondike days. Here is the log-cabin home of Robert W. Service. Here also you may visit various mining operations and see for yourself the "diggings" of the old-time prospectors.

From Dawson you may proceed up the Yukon through the historical Five Finger Rapids where so many of the old-timers lost their lives during the gold-rush days. Then you reach Whitehorse again and will have opportunity to visit the famous Whitehorse Rapids and Miles Canyon.

You may travel by rail from Whitehorse to Carcross, take a steamer for a trip over a beautiful chain of lakes to the renowned Ben-My-Chree homestead on West Taku Arm, then re-entrain at Carcross for Skagway, reversing the historic trek of the early gold seekers, yet you follow their route so closely that at certain points you still may see portions of the old trail.

If you wish to tour throughout Alaska, it is now possible to ship your car by boat to Valdez, southern terminus of the Richardson Highway, and to motor for hundreds of miles through the heart of Alaska. Or you may make the trip by boat, or fly into Valdez' excellent airport, and from there take a bus with connections over the Richardson, Glenn, Steese, and connecting highways; even to Whitehorse and beyond.

From Valdez to Fairbanks, 368 miles, and on to Circle City on the Yukon River, 163 miles, is a thrilling drive for anyone. Most of the distance is through virgin territory and a scenic area of high snow-capped mountains, deep canyons, huge glaciers, and primeval forests, and with occasional glimpses of Alaska's wild life.

Some twenty miles out of Valdez on the Richardson Highway you will cross over Thompson Pass, where the first permanent snowbanks at highway level are observed. Thompson Pass is the forerunner of the awe-inspiring Keystone Canyon, with its breath-taking gorges, above which the highway winds, clinging precariously to the sides of the perpendicular cliffs. Just beyond the pass, alongside the highway, and within camera range is a huge glacier, the first of many such picturesque ice formations to be seen along the highways.

Beyond the Canyon, 116 miles from Valdez, you may turn west onto the Glenn Highway and drive through unexcelled alpine scenery to the Matanuska Valley and Anchorage, a distance of 189 miles from the intersection. Or you may turn east at the 131-mile point onto the Slana-Tok Highway, and drive over the magnificent triangle, with its apex in Tok on the Alaska Highway, and follow the other side of the triangle back to where it again intersects the Richardson Highway. The additional distance to Fairbanks when you follow the triangular route instead of following the Richardson is approximately 110 miles.

There are many branch roads that you may explore if you wish to extend your trip. The Palmer area in the Matanuska Valley is honeycombed with roads, bordered by attractive farms with their neat rows of vegetables and fields of grain, which lead to near-by lakes and recreation areas, also to various interesting mining operations.

A side trip off the Richardson Highway to the little town of Chitina, once headquarters for extensive copper-mining operations, is well worth your while. The road is usually alive with snowshoe rabbits and spruce hens, and as you approach

Chitina, you ride along the edge of a chain of beautiful lakes between picturesque mountains. Chitina is almost a ghost town, once numbering several hundred inhabitants but now containing only a handful. The few remaining residents enjoy modern conveniences in the heart of tremendous mountain ranges.

The Nabesna Road off the Slana-Tok Highway, some sixty miles northeast of where Slana-Tok takes off from the Richardson Highway, is a fascinating forty-four-mile drive to its end at Nabesna. The Elliot Highway from Fairbanks to Livengood, a distance of about eighty miles, penetrates a rugged and picturesque district.

Some wonderful scenery borders the drive beyond Fairbanks along the Steese Highway. Several high passes, which usually are snow-covered in early September, are the routes of migrations of thousands of caribou, and often they are to be seen from the highway. Flocks of ptarmigan—the grouse that turns white in winter—frequent the highway over the high ridges. Near Circle Hot Springs—the fine roadhouse on a branch road from the Steese Highway—and beyond, toward Circle, many foxes are seen along the highway in late summer and early fall, and they can be approached close enough for photographing. (Caution: Rabies is occasionally reported among the foxes, and they should not be approached too closely.)

Travel by air from Fairbanks to Nome, famous gold town of the west coast, is possible and will provide much color and personal contact with one of the most publicized towns in Alaska. From Nome a flight may be made to the Eskimo country of the north—the true Arctic—and you will find much camera material among the Eskimos, with their smiling weather-lined faces and their colorful clothing. They are said to be the most photogenic people in all Alaska, and they are favorite subjects for artists.

In order that there may be no misconception concerning Alaska's highways, it must be understood that they are graveled, two-lane roads, fairly well drained and well bridged, with some quick curves and steep grades. They are comparable to third-grade roads in the States, and a safe speed of only twenty-five to thirty miles per hour may be maintained. The speed limit is thirty-five miles per hour. The Alaska Road Commission has done a remarkably fine job of blasting and digging a foothold for these highways along precipitous sides of tremendous mountain peaks, and it is truly a herculean task to keep them passable. On account of slides and other causes, road repairs are encountered at many points along the highways. Some idea of the task of road building and maintenance in Alaska may be had from the cost of construction—$22,000 per mile—and the annual cost of upkeep—$700 per mile.

Some portions of this highway system are open all the year, but the greater part is closed except during summer and early fall, on account of snowfalls in the mountain passes and glacial conditions along stretches of the highways in the central portion of the Territory.

The Glenn Highway from Anchorage to its connection with the Richardson Highway is usually open all the year. Snow conditions in Thompson Pass out of Valdez usually close that portion of the Richardson Highway in October. Glacial and snow conditions generally close the Richardson south of Fairbanks in October, and the high pass over Eagle Summit on the Steese Highway northeast of Fairbanks requires snow removal in September and closes about October 1. From this brief outline of road conditions it is to be noted that travel over the entire system is possible from about June 15 to October 1, and trips should be arranged accordingly. (Please refer to the Appendix for information concerning the Alaska Highway, Haines Cutoff, and ferry possibilities.)

Motorists throughout Alaska stop and render aid to others in need, because of the distances between stops where service may be had. It is suggested that you adopt this same courtesy toward others when traveling in the Territory.

In all coastal towns of Alaska boat trips are easily arranged, by regular mail boat and by special boats for hire, to hundreds of outlying recreation areas, where hiking trails have been prepared by the Forest Service, aggregating thousands of miles. These trails make accessible lakes, streams, and hunting grounds otherwise practically inaccessible. It is also possible to wander out of any town in southern and southeastern Alaska and follow one of many trails, where the hiker soon finds himself on a lake or stream or vantage point high up on a mountain where he may leisurely drink in the beauty of Alaska's unspoiled wilderness. On week ends and holidays these trails are dotted with hikers, pack boards strapped to their backs, en route to some favored spot for a day or two of refreshing outdoor recreation.

Aside from the convenience offered by Alaska's unlimited coastal waterways in transportation for fishermen, hunters, and hikers to the beginning of coast trails, these waterways offer practically unlimited possibilities both for commercial boat and for pleasure boat trips. An idea of the extent of these possibilities is gained from the length of the coast line measured along its general trend, roughly 6,500 miles, and when the irregularities of its bays, inlets, and fiords are taken into account, the figure is increased to some 26,000 miles.

Every year an increasing number of Alaska visitors both

by private boats and boats for hire are cruising these water-ways, hunting, fishing, and exploring. A leisurely cruise along the southern and southeastern shores of Alaska is the most enjoyable manner of gaining access to the vast territory bordering the waterways, and reveals a stupendous array of cliffs, crags, and magnificent scenery. It is the easiest manner of approach to most of Alaska's big game, and affords the fisherman unlimited opportunities for both salt- and fresh-water fishing. Here, even elderly people or those who do not possess rugged physical qualifications may enjoy Alaska's recreational facilities to the utmost.

Many individually owned boats of all sizes and varying degrees of comforts and accommodations are available in all coastal towns. A letter to the chamber of commerce in any of the coastal towns will bring you the names and addresses of those with boats for hire.

However, the most leisurely and perhaps the most inexpensive manner of traveling throughout interior Alaska today is by railroad and bus. Instead of traveling by boat from the States, you may fly to Anchorage to begin your railroad trip, or to Valdez and reverse the trip, beginning by bus and finishing by rail and boat, or by plane.

Except for brief references to air transportation, this chapter heretofore has dealt largely with ground travel. If you wish to take to the air in Alaska a whole new continent is open to you. Nowhere else on earth is the airplane used so extensively and accepted so nonchalantly by even the most primitive of native peoples.

Much romance has been woven around the bush fliers of Alaska, and some of this romance has gone a bit too far in branding Alaska pilots as devil-may-care air cowboys, who unnecessarily risk both their own and their passengers' necks.

Nothing could be further from the truth. The pilot in Alaska that takes unnecessary risks doesn't last long. However, all pilots take certain risks that cannot be avoided in a land of high mountains and sudden storms.

Among the ranks of Alaska fliers are to be found some of the best pilots on earth, who fly year after year piling up hundreds, even thousands, of hours without serious mishap. These pilots fly all manner of things into places available only by plane. They take food, medicine, and antitoxin into isolated regions and bring out the sick and wounded that need hospitalization. They drop prospectors and trappers down on inland lakes at the beginning of the season and return for them when the season ends. They transport vital mining machinery and tools to inland camps, and make in a matter of hours a trip that by other means would require weeks or months. They fly Eskimo workers from their homes in the north country to the salmon canneries along the coast to alleviate labor shortages, and then fly them back when the season is ended.

Alaska pilots resort to some unusual expedients to deliver emergency messages in rough country where a landing is impossible. The innovation of wadding a message into the cylinder in the middle of a roll of toilet paper is a good illustration. As the roll drops earthward it unrolls, and even if the streamer breaks when the roll hits the ground or snow, the streamer is a good marker and the roll will continue to unroll as it bounces over the terrain and is easy to locate.

These pilots also show an unusual amount of ingenuity in emergency landings, which are sometimes unavoidable. Occasionally the landing is made in an inaccessible region far from a house or settlement, and perhaps the plane's radio is knocked out. Then the pilot, and perhaps a passenger or two, is faced with the problem of waiting for rescue or walking maybe a hundred or more miles across rough, uncharted country without roads or trails, and not infrequently in sub-zero weather. Under such circumstances the exploits of the pilots who make emergency repairs such as using ice to cement parts together, or removing a portion of the propeller in order to make it work, make spectacular reading, and in the telling too much stress is sometimes placed upon the daredeviltry of the pilot that flies the patched plane out, and too little is said about the hazards he and his passengers face if he does not fly it out.

From Dixon Entrance in extreme southeastern Alaska, to the Aleutians in the southwest, following the three-thousand-mile arc of the southern coast line, also northward to Fairbanks and westward to Nome, is a huge continuous chain of improved airfields capable of accommodating all types of commercial and passenger planes. Throughout the whole of Alaska are lakes and rivers with areas sufficient to accommodate float planes in summer, and in the colder areas, ski planes in winter.

Ever increasing thousands are taking advantage of Alaska's splendid air facilities, not only to travel to and from the Territory but to travel within the Territory. For now it is possible to reach isolated districts in an hour or so, in comparative ease and safety; half a century ago such a trip required weeks of hazard and hardship. The Appendix lists Alaska's air carriers.

In planning your trip to Alaska, there is no need for haste. Better accommodations, less congested traffic, and lower costs are in prospect within the next few years.

Alaska's hoaryheaded mountain peaks, mighty sentinels of the sky line, will still be there to greet you. Alaska's aurora, with its brilliant pyrotechnic display, will continue to swish across the winter sky. Alaska's huge glaciers will never give way to the inroads of civilization. Alaska's wild life will remain in abundance for many years to come. Alaska's fiords, those tongues of the sea which extend far up the valleys, with their magnificent scenery will furnish generations yet unborn easy access to Alaska's unlimited recreational resources, to be enjoyed at leisure.

CHAPTER FIVE

Homesteading, Farming,
and Ranching

ALASKA has a particular appeal to the prospective agricultural settler that has inherited an unusual amount of the frontier spirit. But that alone is not enough. He must have a penchant for hard work and be willing to endure some privations, while he, along with others of similar type, are building up the country.

And he should have enough cash to tide him over the first year or two. The amount depends somewhat upon the individual, his ability to shift for himself, how much equipment he brings with him, and where he expects to settle in Alaska. Mr. Don L. Irwin, General Manager, Alaska Rural Rehabilitation Corporation, recommends that a newcomer to the Matanuska Valley have as much as $5,000 to establish himself properly. A recent settler spent $1,300 moving from the States to the valley, $2,300 went for equipment, and an additional $500 was paid down on a tractor. This left him just about a minimum of operating capital from the suggested $5,000.

These figures do not necessarily imply that it is impossible to make a success in Alaska unless the settler has a considerable amount of cash. Many rugged individuals have come to Alaska without much money, have settled on free land, cut the timber and built houses of it, burned the stumps and cultivated the land, and have stayed on it without government or other outside assistance. In emergencies, when short of ready cash, they have worked in Alaska industries, trapped, worked part-time for more established settlers; and with spunk and determination they have carved homes for themselves and their families out of the Alaska wilderness—even as their forefathers did a century ago in the West. These hardy settlers present one of the brightest agricultural pictures in Alaska today.

But the bright side of this picture—the settlers that have made a go of it—is shadowed by the many others who have tried it and failed. Abandoned farms throughout the national forest areas and elsewhere attest to this fact. Even with government financing, over 70 per cent of the original Matanuska Valley settlers found the going too rough, and they were in a favored district and had ample backing.

The fact that one settler fails and another succeeds in Alaska proves conclusively that it is the human factor here, as elsewhere, that makes for success; and the most pronounced qualification for success in Alaska is the frontier spirit—the love of the rough and rugged out-of-doors, grit, determination, ability to absorb hardship, no fear of hard work, experience—without which, with or without cash, a settler is working against heavy odds.

There are several ways to secure a homestead or homesite in Alaska: by direct purchase from someone who has title; by complying with requirements for homesteading; by leasing acreage; or by purchasing a homesite from the government. District land offices are maintained in Anchorage, Fairbanks, and Nome. Information concerning areas available for entry in the public domain, which covers approximately 90 per cent of the land area of Alaska, may be obtained from any of these district offices or from the Commissioner, General Land

Office, Washington 25, D.C. Information regarding land in a national forest—national forests constitute about 5.5 per cent of the land area—may be secured from the Regional Forester, U.S. Forest Service, Juneau, Alaska.

In general, to secure land under homesite or homestead regulations an applicant must be twenty-one years of age or the head of a family, a citizen of the United States or have declared his intention to become a citizen, and must not be the owner of more than 160 acres of land in the United States, except that a homestead entry made in the United States outside of Alaska is not a disqualification.

Maximum acreage to be obtained under the homestead law is 160 acres. The first step in acquiring a homestead is to make a settlement on the land or to file an application for a homestead entry at the appropriate land office. A claim may be initiated by settlement on either surveyed or unsurveyed land, but application for entry can be filed for surveyed land only.

Settlement means actually going upon the land with the intention of using it as a home. A settler on unsurveyed land should mark the boundaries of the land claimed, post a notice of his claim thereon, and have a notice of his location recorded with the United States Commissioner of the proper recording district within ninety days after date of settlement. In this way he protects himself against adverse claims or efforts of others to acquire the same land. After the settler has remained on the land for seven months out of each year for three years, and has complied with other requirements explained below, he is entitled to have his land surveyed free of charge. Within three months after the official filing of a plat of survey, the person should make formal homestead entry of the land settled upon.

If a settler wishes to acquire a homestead of surveyed land, his claim must be initiated by filing with the appropriate district office, within ninety days of date of settlement, an application to make homestead entry. Blank forms may be obtained from the nearest district office.

Residence must begin within six months after the entry is granted, and a claimant must live thereon not less than seven months per year during each of three years. He and his family, on both surveyed and unsurveyed land, must live on the land during this period, must have under cultivation at least one-sixteenth of the land by the end of the second year of his entry, or settlement if unsurveyed, and one-eighth each year thereafter until submission of final proof; and he must have a habitable house upon the land at the time of proof.

A homesteader is not required to live continuously upon the land after he has established his residence, provided his family remains there as required by law. This permits a homesteader to take advantage of outside gainful employment while he is legitimately homesteading his land.

Instead of residence of seven months per year for three years, the homesteader may reside six months a year for four years; five months a year for five years; or, after fourteen months of continuous residence, he may commute and pay a fee of $1.25 per acre in order to gain immediate possession.

There is a total cost for fees, advertising, and so forth, of from $35.00 to $50.00 in connection with homesteading, plus the $1.25 per acre mentioned above if the settler wishes to commute instead of remaining on the land the full time required.

In general, the lands which now offer the best prospects for agricultural settlement will be found in the Tanana River Valley near Fairbanks, in the Cook Inlet–Matanuska Valley area of southern Alaska, and on the Kenai Peninsula. When

Alaska's hoaryheaded mountain peaks, sentinels of the sky line, will be there always to greet the visitor.

Tongues of the sea extend many miles inland from Alaska's coast line and provide easy access to hunting, fishing, and other outdoor sports. (*Copyright The Snap Shop*)

Waterfall in Southeastern Alaska. Clear mountain streams and forested hills delight the eye of the tourist. (*Copyright Forest Service*)

During the salmon season bears frequent the streams to feed on the spawning fish. Instead of knocking the fish from the water with a paw, as often portrayed, bears nearly always catch fish with their teeth. (*Copyright The Alaska Sportsman*)

Glaciers represent nature in one of its most spectacular and awe-inspiring aspects.

Lupine blossoms at Mendenhall Glacier. Summer brings a riot of color to Alaska's valleys and mountainsides. (*Copyright Forest Service*)

Trappers returning to civilization after a season in Alaska wilds. The airplane is more extensively used in the Territory than anywhere else on earth. (*Copyright The Alaska Sportsman*)

Hundreds of inland lakes, such as Lake Reflection, provide landing facilities for float planes. (*Copyright Forest Service*)

roads now under construction are completed, it is believed that lands along the eastern shore of Cook Inlet, near Homer, will be especially desirable, owing to the mildness of the winters, ample rainfall, and good agricultural soil. Nearly every homestead in the Homer area has its own coal mine for fuel. However, the most favorable land in this area is rapidly being taken up, and a large proportion of it already is under settlement.

The Kuskokwim and Yukon valleys have millions of acres of potential agricultural land, and there are vast acreages between the Tanana and Fortymile rivers; but they offer little immediate possibilities, because of their inaccessibility. The prospective settler should keep abreast of road construction in these areas, as it is possible that connections with the Alaska and other highways may open up some of these districts.

Anyone that does not expect to follow agriculture for a livelihood may obtain five acres or less, suitable for a home and garden, by purchase from the government if he lives on the land in a habitable house for five months out of each year for three years. The price of land thus acquired is $2.50 per acre, with a minimum of $10.00.

Public lands may also be acquired by lease from the government for manufacturing sites, for grazing, fur farming, and so forth. All such grants require occupancy within a reasonable stated time.

A comprehensive pamphlet entitled *Answers to Questions by Servicemen about Land Settlement in Alaska* may be obtained from the General Land Office, Washington 25, D.C. It is printed in question-and-answer form and contains information valuable not only to servicemen but also to any other prospective Alaska homesteader.

The question of credit on homesteading in Alaska for time spent in military service during war is answered in this pamphlet, to the effect that time served in World War I and previous wars and campaigns, up to two years, is allowed. In other words, an ex-serviceman who has served two years in previous wars can homestead land in Alaska with a three-year resident requirement, and his war credit will cut this to one year, provided that he establishes residence and cultivates the required portion of land. Thus a serviceman with two years' service can stay on the land seven months and acquire title to it. Since that pamphlet was published, a bill H. R. 5025 has been passed extending the same privilege to veterans of World War II.

There never has been much question about the ability of Alaska's soil to produce bountiful crops of grain and produce, or the adaptability of its climate for production of poultry and livestock. The question has been one of accessibility to markets. The Matanuska Valley offers perhaps the best market of any portion of Alaska.

Importation of 201 families into the Matanuska Valley by the government-owned Alaska Rural Rehabilitation Corporation in 1935 was a national event and has created much controversy. So much has been written about this project that nearly everybody in the States now holds to one of two opinions: that the whole thing was impractical in its conception, impossible in its operation, and prohibitive in its cost; or that the abundant crops from the valley that furnished food for construction workers and Army personnel, and the more recent "million-dollar crops" harvested there, have proved the practicability of the project. Neither of these opinions is entirely correct.

The avowed purpose of the Matanuska Valley Project was rehabilitation of the afore-mentioned 201 families from the drought-stricken regions in the States. The project was only partially successful in accomplishing that purpose. It was inevitable that group importation of agricultural settlers into a new country such as Alaska, without too much consideration for the frontier spirit and other necessary qualifications, would meet with only mediocre success. Dissatisfaction, bitterness, and abandonment of farms by the unfit were unavoidable.

And while it is true that war brought a demand and a high price for everything that could be raised in the valley, it also brought a cry for workers on construction jobs at $1.75 per hour, which encouraged abandonment in favor of war work.

It is irrefutable that the cost of the Matanuska colonization program was absolutely prohibitive except to a benign government with a supposedly bottomless moneybag. And it is equally true that many people in the States look askance at any co-operative association, such as the government-directed program in the Matanuska Valley, if it appears to compete with independent American industry, and if any American loses any of his rugged individualism in favor of collectivism. The true frontiersman has always sought individual freedom for individual effort, and has expected nothing more than success or failure as merited by his own efforts.

As the misfits and malcontents were gradually weeded out and replaced by more suitable settlers, and the frontier-spirited proportion of the original settlers got their feet on the ground, Matanuska gradually improved. The thriving settlement of today bears little resemblance to the hodgepodge of disillusioned, discontented, bickering colonists of its first few years of existence.

No discussion of Matanuska would be complete without mentioning that a goodly proportion of the settlers in the Matanuska Valley are old-timers that were there before the government settlement was established.

The people in the valley enjoy a great many co-operative improvements built by the Rehabilitation Corporation, including a fine school, dormitory, hospital, trading post, creamery, garage, warehouse, powerhouse, and meat kitchen. The holdings of the Rehabilitation Corporation were sold to the Matanuska Valley Farmers Co-operative Association in January 1940, which since has added potato storage, cabinet shop, grading and processing of produce, a dairy in Anchorage, slaughterhouse, and other advantages. The Co-operative Association has about 150 members and is a nonprofit corporation. It is functioning today as an independent organization, successfully marketing the products of its members and keeping them fairly well in line in the matter of selling only through the "Co-op"; however, it still is under the watchful eye of the Rehabilitation Corporation and other government agencies that hold mortgages totaling its approximate worth.

Of the original 201 families that came to the valley in 1935, 58 remained after ten years, at which time there were 170 families in the colony, including replacements. The cost of the project was said to be about $5,000,000 (some say much more), or approximately $30,000 per family based on the 170 families which still were in the colony after ten years. This, however, is hardly a fair figure when one considers that the $5,000,000 has built approximately $1,000,000 worth of roads, the school, and has made other improvements in the district that are enjoyed by all of the valley settlers, comprising some 300 families.

Most of the colonists owed about $7,500 each for farms

and for money borrowed to get started. Twelve of them have paid all they owe.

Some of the finest small farms to be seen anywhere under the American flag are in the valley, and a visitor is indeed calloused if he does not share with the owners to some extent the feeling of pride of accomplishment when he views one of these prosperous, well-kept farms with all its buildings—the inevitable result of hard work.

One cannot value the success and happiness of families in mere dollars, particularly if the money is expended to give them the opportunity for success.

Farming in the valley is most profitable if largely confined to dairying, poultry, livestock, and produce. Eggs, milk, and potatoes have been profitable crops, and a good market usually has prevailed, except that potatoes occasionally become a drug on the market because of overproduction for local consumption and inability to compete in outside markets.

Many co-operative advantages, aside from marketing, are available in the valley, such as clearing land, breaking and tilling the soil, well drilling, and so forth. The Rehabilitation Corporation charges reasonable hourly rates for man and machine for breaking land, bulldozing trees and stumps from new land, tilling, and well drilling. Work is done in order, but with preference given old settlers. If a farmer has security and proves that he is dependable and honest, short-term loans are available to him in the Matanuska area from the Matanuska Valley Co-operative Association and the Alaska Rural Rehabilitation Corporation, as well as from banks and other sources in Alaska.

An experiment station of the University of Alaska is situated in the Matanuska Valley. Work consists of animal husbandry, entomology, and crop experimentation. Crops in the valley are free from many pests common to the States, but sporadic infestation of cutworms causes very great damage to nearly all crops, and the root maggot is seriously affecting all of the mustard family—cabbage, turnips, and so forth. Corrosive sublimate helps control this pest but is not 100-percent effective.

Certain warm-weather crops, such as tomatoes and cucumbers, which do not produce well in the open field in Alaska, produce abundantly in the experimental station greenhouse and in many privately owned greenhouses throughout the Territory. Greenhouse tomatoes produce in such profusion that they grow in clusters not unlike grapes.

The experiment station has an annual field day in September, when farmers gather from throughout the valley and are given the benefit of the results of the year's experiments. Lectures by the personnel of the station, by visiting members of the university staff, and by visiting Rehabilitation Corporation officials are well attended. Lunch on the ground, with field games, adds a picnic touch to the meeting.

A tour of the produce gardens, fields, and through the animal shelters, conducted by different members of the staff, brings to the interested farmers a firsthand account, together with substantiating exhibits, of the results of experiments. An illustration in animal husbandry is the established fact that when salmon oil (vitamins A and D), easily procurable in the Territory, is fed to ewes at the station, they produce healthier lambs and more pairs of lambs.

The Matanuska Valley has more than eight thousand acres cleared and in cultivation, and this is being increased yearly. There is a little land still available for homesteading in the valley outside the colony, but this is going fast. Land in the colony in blocks of forty to a hundred acres may be purchased through the General Manager, Alaska Rural Rehabilitation Corporation, Palmer, Alaska. When a farm becomes vacant, the ARRC will sell, either for cash or not less than 25 per cent down, the balance on amortization payments with 3 per cent interest on unpaid balance, payable within fifteen years.

The prices of these farms range from $4,500 to $6,000, depending upon the number of acres of cleared land, kind and condition of buildings, and other factors such as topography, distance from town, and so forth. Most farms have from twenty to forty acres of cleared land, and the buildings include a large barn, well and well house, and possibly additional small buildings. In some instances, government land is adjacent or near by.

Purchase can also be made from private owners, usually farmers. In such cases the sale is negotiated directly with the owner. Occasionally a purchase can be made of a farm fully equipped with machinery, livestock, furniture, and all. Many farmhouses are equipped with furnaces, electricity, and running water; barns with cement floors, stanchions, drinking cups, and electric power. Some farms have silos, modern milkhouses, and well-equipped poultry houses.

Forested land, naturally, has to be cleared. And clearing land in Alaska is always an expensive procedure, costing from $125 to more than $1,000 per acre, depending upon the locality, topography, and timber coverage. Timber is cut and sold or used for building and firewood; the stumps usually are allowed to rot in the ground until the second year, when a bulldozer is employed to uproot them. It takes more time to bulldoze green stumps, and a great deal more soil is lost in the uprooting. In and near the Matanuska Valley this bulldozing is done at an hourly rate, and a bulldozer usually is available.

Alaska soil varies from silt loam to fine sand, with varying quantities of vegetable matter in different stages of decomposition intermixed.

A very complete mimeographed question-and-answer folder has been prepared by Mr. Don L. Irwin, General Manager, Alaska Rural Rehabilitation Corporation, Palmer, Alaska, concerning the obtaining of land in the valley. This folder is available upon request.

The next most highly developed farming area in Alaska is the Tanana River Valley near Fairbanks, where some land is available for purchase from individuals, and a great deal is available for settlement. An experimental station is also located not far from Fairbanks at the University of Alaska. Here more individual effort is required, and more independence in marketing is employed. Many beautiful farms dot the valley near Fairbanks, and a good local market is available at present for nearly everything the farm produces.

Principal types of farming throughout Alaska are dairying, general farming, truck farming, and hog, cattle, or poultry raising.

Because of variations in soil types and topography throughout the farming areas of Alaska, there is little actual farming as it is known throughout the broad, level farmlands of the States, where field crops are the money crops, and vegetables, poultry, and milk usually are produced to augment the field-crop income. Most successful farmers in Alaska produce field crops for feed for livestock and poultry, which together with potatoes and other vegetables constitute the money crop.

Many kinds of vegetables grow luxuriantly. The excellent quality and flavor are due to the fertility and suitable texture of the soil and to atmospheric conditions, such as ample moisture, cool temperatures, and long days. These vegetables include radishes, leaf and head lettuce, early and late cabbage, cauliflower, parsnips, celery, rutabagas, turnips, carrots, beets, chard, string beans, rhubarb, peas, onions, kohlrabi, and spinach. The Petrosky variety of turnip is notably high in quality. Many varieties of potatoes (White Bliss, Arctic Seedling, White Gold, Early Ohio, Green Mountain, Katahdin, and others) grow well. The Arctic Seedling appears to hold the edge as a preference. Pen Lake lettuce, New York 12, and Imperial 44 do well.

Several varieties of canning peas do particularly well in Alaska. Garden peas of unusually fine flavor and high yields are available for the table throughout the spring, summer, and early fall.

Crops grown are oats, barley, wheat, peas, grasses, and legumes.

The varieties of oats usually grown are Victory, Climax, Gopher, and Swedish Select. From a seeding of seventy-five to a hundred pounds per acre an average yield of about forty-five bushels per acre is secured. An application of a hundred pounds per acre of treble superphosphate is considered profitable by many farmers.

Both hull-less and hulled varieties of barley are grown; hull-less 19-B variety, White Hull-less, and Manchurian are usually planted. From a seeding of eighty pounds per acre the yield is usually about twenty-three bushels per acre.

The main type of wheat is the Siberian or Chogot variety. This is a spring wheat; winter-wheat varieties are seldom grown. Seeding of eighty pounds per acre, with an application of about a hundred pounds of commercial fertilizer, yields about twenty-two bushels per acre.

Oats and field peas, with barley sometimes added, make an excellent silage crop. Alsike clover, yellow-flowered alfalfa, white clover, and yellow sweet clover, together with several varieties of grasses, are mowed the first part of July, at which time suitable weather is usually available. A wide variety of perennial grasses and a few legumes are suitable for pasture for cattle, sheep, and horses.

Bush fruits, such as currants, gooseberries, and red raspberries, produce large yields of excellent quality. Strawberries are large and of good flavor. Wild berries are to be found everywhere in the woods and mountains, including currants, raspberries, high-bush cranberries, low-bush cranberries, and blueberries. A gastronomic treat often seen on settlers' tables in Alaska is moose or caribou meat served with spiced cranberries and freshly cooked vegetables.

Winters in the Fairbanks farming area are extremely cold, and the growing season short. However, the number of hours of sunlight—twenty to twenty-two a day in midsummer—produces remarkably rapid growth and maturity of crops. Rainfall is light in this area, but ample for crop-growing needs.

In the Matanuska Valley the winters are very much less severe, and the growing season longer. Rainfall likewise is heavier.

Shelter for livestock is essential. However, heating is seldom needed even in the Fairbanks area, and not at all throughout the Cook Inlet area of southern Alaska nor in southeastern Alaska. Smudge fires, burlap or wire screening, and insecticides during the mosquito season of spring and early summer are used for protection of livestock in some sections. Farmers wear head nets and canvas gloves when working in fields during the worst of the mosquito season, especially if the land is near a brushy area.

The clearing of lands, draining of swamplands, and development of pastures have greatly reduced mosquito infestation in the Matanuska Valley and other portions of the Territory. More powerful and longer-lasting insect sprays now offer invaluable relief to man and beast in Alaska.

Southeastern Alaska has only limited agricultural possibilities because of its mountainous terrain and the excessive expense— from $600 to $1,200 an acre—of clearing the luxuriant growth of moss, brush, and trees, and because of the prevalence of fallen timber. This is the area in which fallen timber does not decay quickly on account of the excess moisture and cool climate in both summer and winter.

Many varieties of vegetables and fruits, including carrots, rutabagas, cabbages, and potatoes, also strawberries and raspberries, are raised in numerous small plots throughout southeastern Alaska and produce abundantly. Dairy farming is practicable in some districts, and a ready market is available in near-by towns. In recent years, apples, plums, and cherries have been produced successfully in the Ketchikan area. Thus far the supply has been limited to owner consumption, and the possibilities for commercial production have not been convincingly established.

Chickens, turkeys, geese, and ducks are produced throughout most of Alaska, and there is considerable demand for both eggs and meat. Chicken-and-egg production is fast becoming a leading agricultural industry, especially in the Matanuska Valley. The most common breeds of chickens raised at present are White Leghorn, Hampshire Red, Rhode Island Red, and Barred Rock.

Most every farm has a few hogs. A number of farms have their own curing houses, and many farmers in the valley utilize the Co-operative Association slaughterhouse for butchering hogs as well as other kinds of livestock.

Although the demand for meat far exceeds the local supply,

cattle and sheep raising has not progressed to any marked extent in Alaska. There are many good reasons why Alaska does not produce its own meat. First and foremost: Nowhere in Alaska can government-owned land be purchased in sufficient acreage to enable cattle production on a profitable basis. Even if two homesteaders settle on adjoining land, their total acreage is 320—not enough for any reasonable cattle production except as an adjunct to farming. And two families would have to subsist upon it. Land can be leased, yes—for a period of twenty years, but cannot be purchased. In view of this, and the fact that a considerable investment is required for cattle ranching in Alaska, as elsewhere, ranchers will probably continue to pass up the Territory as a potential cattle-raising country in favor of ranching in the States where land in sufficient blocks may still be purchased outright, improved, and handed down from generation to generation, in the good American way.

Alaska possesses hundreds of square miles suitable for ranching, if such land could be privately owned, fenced, proper shelter provided for livestock, and predatory animals destroyed. The Alaska Peninsula, Kodiak Island, the Aleutians, and other grass-covered portions of the coast offer possibilities for livestock. One of the largest dairies in Alaska—a hundred cows—is located on Kodiak. Sheep are produced in this area, but from all reports such production is on a more or less haphazard basis. A flock of about 2,500 sheep is allowed to roam almost at will on the little island of Chernfski near the Aleutians, west of Kodiak. On this island the weather is comparatively mild with little snow in winter. Natives help shear the flock, which requires little attention otherwise. About twelve pounds of wool per sheep per year has been clipped from the flock; however, little utilization of meat is reported. Sheep in this area are said to be so well fleeced that they often are subject to wool blindness.

The most heavily populated area, southeastern Alaska, is so near Seattle that meat can be imported cheaper than it can be produced locally, owing to Alaska's higher wage scale, limited pasturage, and so forth.

The best opportunity for cattle raising, when (if ever) the government decides to sell land to individuals in sufficient blocks for successful ranching, appears to be from Anchorage north along the Alaska Railroad. This district is from 1,700 to 2,000 miles from Seattle, and with the usual high boat and railroad rates from Seattle on refrigerated fresh meat, there is somewhat of a protective tariff in favor of locally produced meat. It has an advantage over the afore-mentioned island areas as its railroad and highway facilities offer a wide distribution into districts of rapidly expanding population. From the upper Cook Inlet–Matanuska region to the Tanana Valley around Fairbanks is a region that will bear investigation by interested cattlemen.

This area produces considerable forage on the open range. A herd of buffalo in the Big Delta area has increased from an original stock of twenty-five, placed there some fifteen years ago, to an estimated four hundred head, without any winter feeding whatsoever. Two horses that went astray east of Palmer several years ago were recovered—one a year later and the other two years later—little the worse for the time spent on the loose. Cattle, however, cannot be permitted on the open range without some protection from the weather, especially in the interior, and from predatory animals. Recently a rancher shipped a carload of heifers into Palmer with the intention of ranging them on government land on the slopes of the mountains lying east and north of the Matanuska Valley. Within a week three of the heifers were killed by bears, and the remainder were hastily rounded up and transported to safer pastures.

Green feed for winter use—oats, peas, vetch, and so forth, for storage in trench silos—and ripened grain for fattening can be successfully grown throughout the railroad area.

Herefords are specially adapted for the colder Fairbanks district; Guernseys and Holsteins are the preferred dairy breeds. When a highway is available from the States, trucking in of original stocks from the States and from northern Alberta is worthy of consideration.

The rancher or agricultural settler who expects to make his home in Alaska should first make a trip to a desirable area, and thus learn firsthand what the possibilities are for success. It is most advisable to make all arrangements for a farm to occupy before moving his family, livestock, and equipment to Alaska. Usually such things as hay, seed, and fertilizer can be purchased in the well-established farming areas, and from January to March is considered a desirable time to occupy a new home and arrange for these farm supplies.

He should ship his tractor, plows, and other farm equipment; also his household furniture, and the kind of livestock and poultry he wishes to raise. Only high-quality stock should be brought in, as it is almost impossible to purchase good breeding stock in Alaska, and it costs no more to ship fine stock than poor stock.

A farm truck, three-quarter-ton to ton-and-a-half, should be included. Some threshing and feed grinding, in addition to tractor work, is available in the better farming areas of Alaska.

Information on settlers' rates may be obtained from the Alaska Steamship Company, Seattle, Washington.

If any of this discussion of farming and ranching possibilities in Alaska indicates the need for haste on the part of prospective settlers in order to secure favorable locations while they still are available, that impression should be corrected. It is true that the most favorable locations in well-established areas are being settled rapidly. However, it should be mentioned again that roads now under construction and on the agenda for immediate construction as soon as funds are available will open up new agricultural areas probably as good, maybe better, than those which now are being settled. Further, there is nothing to indicate that abandonment of farms by the unfit will not continue as heretofore, thus making available these improved farms.

There is no need for hurried exploitation of Alaska's agricultural possibilities, and for that reason only those that feel themselves fully qualified to make a success of it, and that have the urge to pit their efforts against frontier conditions in this big, rugged country, should attempt it.

Prospective ranchers might even profit by delay. For surely someone in Washington with authority must realize, sooner or later, that the American people do not wish to lease land, and that nonproductive government-owned land in Alaska, of which there is an abundance, will assume its proper productiveness only when it is sold to and improved by a good American rancher. No greater satisfaction can come to the individual American than that which permeates his soul when he looks over his broad acres and says, "This is my land." Pride of ownership is his inherited characteristic.

It is not at all probable that the government will experiment with another such project as Matanuska. Nearly three years after the establishment of that project the following quotation occurred in the government booklet *Regional Planning— Alaska, Its Resources and Development*:

> Obviously, the United States proper does not need Alaska as an outlet for a surplus population. . . . Alaska is not needed as a potential means of satisfying the land-hunger of the American people. . . . It may be suggested that with vast areas in the United States subject to drought conditions and other hazards, with substantial amounts of land of marginal or sub-marginal character, and with fewer opportunities for the small operator to profit from exploitation of land resources, Alaska offers a new frontier. No doubt in a limited sense Alaska does provide some opportunity of this character, but as a solution to a problem which may exist in the continental United States, it must be dropped from consideration. No emergency condition exists that demands drastic action and there appears to be no necessity or desirability for applying any "forced-feeding" process to induce agricultural development.

Nowhere in Alaska can a settler unload his plow and begin turning rich, level prairie land—an advantage enjoyed by our forefathers who settled portions of the prairie sections of the West. If however he is willing to work and undergo hardship and the usual privations of getting started in a fine new country, he will find in Alaska the opportunity to rear his family in the clean environment of the great out-of-doors and with education for his children in first-class schools, picture shows and other entertainment in near-by towns, co-operative neighbors, and a helping hand extended to him from many government agencies as well as from the experimental stations of the University of Alaska.

The mountains and wooded valleys near by afford year-round recreation for him and his family—picnicking, fishing, boating, hiking, picture taking, hunting, berrypicking, mountain climbing, skating, and skiing.

And he soon will learn to love Alaska.

CHAPTER SIX

Trapping and Fur Farming

FROM the time Vitus Bering discovered Alaska in 1741, furs have been one of the Territory's principal exports. In fact, it was the abundance and variety of fur-bearing animals that attracted the attention of early explorers to these sparsely tenanted shores. Glowing accounts brought back by the survivors of Bering's expedition and by venturesome Siberian traders, substantiated by piles of luxurious pelts taken during those brief forays, brought the first exploiters and settlers to Alaska.

The romantic early history of Alaska is the history of the Russian-American Company and lesser organizations in their quest for furs; and even today, interesting stories come out of this vast northland of the lonely trapper in his isolated cabin, garnering rich pelts from his wilderness trap line. The story of Alaska is thoroughly interwoven with the romance of furs.

The reports of those early-day Russian explorers are replete with vivid accounts of innumerable sea otters playing along the beaches, of literally millions of fur seals from the Pribilof Island rookeries, migrating back and forth through the Aleutians; of shore and forest teeming with mink, marten, land otter, weasel, fox, lynx, muskrat, beaver, and other fur bearers.

The chief prize sought after by those early explorers and traders was the lustrous fur of the sea otter, always one of the most precious of furs. The last pelts taken sold for more than two thousand dollars each. The color of the fur is sometimes a pale grayish-brown, but the best skins are almost black. Sometimes the long hairs in these dark skins are tipped with silver, and then the fur is indeed worth a king's ransom. The long hairs of the sea otter are very soft and silky, and unlike the skins of other water animals, they do not have to be plucked out when the fur is being prepared for use.

These lovable creatures, whose habitat is the kelp beds surrounding the islands of the Alaska Peninsula and the Aleutian chain, are perhaps the most charming, intelligent, and harmless animals on earth. Their almost human characteristics entitle them to a place apart in the animal kingdom.

Strange tales are handed down from the old explorers of how sea otters show near-human affection for each other, the mated pairs caressing and fondling each other in a most lover-like manner. The mother likewise is said to display her affection for her baby by kissing, caressing, bouncing it up and down to quiet its whimpering, and romping with it in a playful manner, much as a woman fondles her child.

The young of the sea otter cannot swim, and the mother carries it on her breast while swimming on her back. If left alone too long, the baby will thrash about and soon drown. As the baby matures, he is taught to swim by the simple expedient of leaving him alone for longer intervals, until his frantic efforts to reach the protection of his mother are finally rewarded by a few successful strokes. Gradually he becomes almost as expert at aquatic sports as the fishes.

Groups of sea otters romp and play in the water very much like a group of half-grown boys in the old swimming hole. Mr. Jack O'Connor of the Alaska Game Commission says that he has watched some of them at play. Sometimes they play ball by tossing a bit of seaweed or other flotsam from one to the other.

An interesting habit of the sea otter, which may have given rise to the mermaid legend, is his manner of raising himself up in the water until about half of his body is exposed, then gazing about the horizon with his handlike paw up against his brow to shade his eyes, as he scans the water for enemies.

When the Russians first discovered these quaint animals, they were said to be quite tame and would come scrambling over the rocks to meet their visitors, fawning about their feet like young puppies. Hunters clubbed them to death by the hundreds, for instead of attempting to escape they would cover their heads with their paws and stand with a look of bewilderment.

Such indiscriminate slaughter continued until the sea otter was believed to be entirely extinct. In recent years, however, a few were discovered in the far reaches of the Aleutian Islands. Rigid protection has increased their numbers until there are now several thousand of them along the fogbound, rocky shores. There is a marked difference in the demeanor of these few surviving sea otters from that of the original vast herds. From cruel experience, the offspring of those tame, friendly creatures have become wild and almost unapproachable.

Lovers of wild life will be pleased to learn that the Japanese destruction, during their occupancy of some of this island chain, of seal and sea-otter herds did not occur to such an extent as was feared. A letter from the United States Department of the Interior, after the Japs had been expelled from the islands, reads in part as follows:

For your information, the fur-seal herds along the Aleutians seem to have suffered little damage as results of the war. The Government of the United States figures that it will take more seal skins this year than have been taken for a number of years, as the Japanese have made no inroads on the seals. [A record catch of more than 75,000 skins was taken in one year, bearing out the prediction.] The seals leave the Pribilof Islands in the early fall on the first storms in September, and return to those islands about early May. In this way they missed the Japs who were located on a few of the Aleutians Islands.

As to the sea otters, we will probably never know how many the Japs got. Some of the sea otters may have been killed by bombs exploding in the water, or shell fire during patrols. There is also a loss where the otters come in contact with patches of oil floating on the kelp beds; their fur becomes so matted with oil that the animal dies. While this can be attributed to the war, it is hard to place the blame on anyone for the presence of oil along the coast.

Fur seals, like the sea otters, were slaughtered to near extinction until recent years, when the United States Government, under an agreement with Russia, Japan, and Great Britain wherein each would have a portion of the fur-seal take, took over the killing of seals. However, Japan repudiated the fur-seal treaty sixty days before Pearl Harbor.

Under rigid protection, all breeding stock is unmolested. Coast Guard cutters escort the seals in their annual migrations to the Pribilofs, where three-year-olds, called "bachelors," are singled out for slaughter. Many Alaska natives are employed by the government in this controlled sealing industry. The pelts are taken and prepared for market under government auspices, and only then is the division of the catch made with the other interested nations. This planned killing of only the three-year-olds has increased the herd from a low of 135,000 to an estimated 3,100,000—almost as many as there were when we purchased Alaska from Russia in 1867, and the total value of skins taken about equals the purchase price paid for Alaska.

It is said that between six and seven sealskins are required for a single coat, therefore the recent record catch will make some ten thousand ladies' coats.

Fur animals of Alaska are the basis of the major part of the income of hundreds of Indians, Eskimos, and Aleuts, as well as many white trappers throughout the Territory. While many of these trappers have developed other ways of supplementing their livelihood, still, trapping, hunting, and fishing must be the mainstay of their existence for many years to come. Fur trapping affords seasonal employment for nearly twenty thousand people, including natives, and provides normally more than two million dollars in income. With present high prices the crop is providing much more than the usual income. Many homesteaders and old-timers, as well as professional trappers, measure good times by the number and prices of the furs taken.

Moving to Alaska for a life of Daniel Boone is not usually encouraged. But with the present demand for furs and the unusually high prices now in effect, Daniel Boone undoubtedly could get rich if he were in Alaska today. Mink is bringing the highest price obtained in fifteen years. Marten, ermine, and otter likewise are in demand. Beaver and muskrat are in good demand and the price is high.

Until the war came along it was the consensus that Alaska

was already being trapped pretty thoroughly, and every species of fur animal was being cropped as closely as was consistent with maintaining a safe breeding supply. Now, however, with the increase in recent years of wolves and coyotes and with the present high bounties (see Appendix) trapping of fur-bearing animals as an adjunct to wolf trapping might offer an adequate income to an expert trapper. New settlers frequently trap near their recently acquired homesteads to augment scanty incomes during the first year or two of clearing land and planting crops. Many commercial fishermen turn to trapping during the winter months.

Throughout central and north central Alaska are many trappers that have other vocations. Some are civil engineers, some doctors, and many of them are well qualified to make a living in other ways than trapping, but they like it. There is something about the vast snowy silences of the north country that gets into a man's blood. Some people marvel at the make-up of a man who can be content with the solitude, the loneliness, and the biting cold. But as a matter of fact, a trapper is a pretty busy man. He often has his traps strung out over a line twenty or thirty miles long, with a cabin or two along the route, and he knows that if he is to be successful he must make the route at reasonably regular intervals, else a wandering wolverine or other predator is likely to relieve him of his catch. Then he must thaw out the animal, skin it, clean the surplus fat and meat particles from the hide, stretch and treat it. And there are the chores of changing sets and procuring trap bait.

If the trapper is alone, he must keep his fire going, prepare his own meals, and attend to the hundreds of other little household duties that help keep him comfortable.

One such "avocational frontiersman" in central Alaska is

by profession a skilled and experienced dentist. For two years or more he has lived in his well-appointed and well-kept cabin on the bank of a large lake. In summer he guides fishing parties, transporting them to choice spots in his fast boats. Many of these parties are his friends, whom he guides without charge. In winter he does a certain amount of trapping—not enough to make too much of a task of it. He lives alone in winter in a vast area of perhaps a hundred square miles, and aside from a couple of trappers several miles away, his books, radio, and telephone are his sole winter companions.

The number of these avocational frontiersmen—men well educated and well qualified for other vocations who trap, prospect, and live alone in the great out-of-doors simply because they like it—will surprise the newcomer.

Because of excessive trapping without regulation until recent years, rigid closed seasons are enforced throughout Alaska, and in some districts there is no open season on certain species. From the outline of fur districts and seasons (see Appendix), it is clear that in all parts of Alaska valuable pelts may be taken in season. For more detailed information, the current regulatory announcement may be secured free from the Alaska Game Commission, Juneau, Alaska.

It will be of interest to prospective settlers who wish to pit their trapping and hunting knowledge against the cunning of Alaska wolves and coyotes, that Fur District 7 offers good opportunities for both wolves and fur-bearing animals, especially foxes. This district is one of extreme cold in winter, and to work in it one must have knowledge of how to cope with arctic temperatures as well as how to hunt and trap.

Epizootic diseases that kill untold numbers of rodents and other small animals and game birds at recurring intervals, when ranges become too crowded, cause a shortage of foxes and other animals that feed upon the life subject to such diseases. Because of these periodic shortages, it is sometimes necessary to close the season in a district until the fur bearers stage a comeback. While it has not been found necessary to close any district on all fur bearers, this phenomenon of plenty followed by shortage has encouraged the establishment of commercial fur farms in Alaska. These farms, when isolated from wild animals, are not so subject to such diseases.

The islands of the southern coast are particularly adaptable to fur farming, and in some districts it is fairly well established. In addition to the fur crop, breeding animals are sold each year to purchasers all over the world. About half the fur farmers are more interested in minks than in other fur bearers, while silver foxes are next in importance.

Fish, a satisfactory basic food for fur bearers, is abundant and easily obtained. The climate is also favorable for the production of high-grade furs, for which Alaska is justly famous, and for which the prices are good.

Ranchers are experimenting with marten, beaver, fox, land otter, fitch, raccoon, and muskrat. The University of Alaska has an experimental station at Petersburg, where, in connection with the Fish and Wildlife Service, various projects in relation to Alaska fur farming are being carried out. Here recently marten were reproduced successfully in captivity.

Ample locally produced breeding stock is available for the equipping of fur ranches. The Alaska Game Commission at Juneau maintains a list of all licensed fur farmers, which will be mailed free to persons interested.

To obtain fur-farm leases within the Tongass or Chugach National Forests, application must be made to the Forest Service office in Juneau. Leases of land in the national forests for fur-farming purposes may be obtained for islands up to one thousand acres in extent, or for tracts on the mainland of not more than eighty acres. Permits authorize the use of the land for a period not to exceed twenty years; however, renewals are possible after expiration of lease. Applicants for fur-farm leases must show proof of financial ability to carry on such operations, in addition to making initial improvements. Permittees are required within a reasonable time to place four pairs of animals on islands up to five hundred acres, or seven pairs on islands between five hundred and a thousand acres. All fur-farm rentals are subject to adjustment at five-year intervals.

The approved rates at present are $12.50 per year for islands under five hundred acres, and $25.00 per year for islands between five hundred and a thousand acres. For mainland areas, the rates are $5.00 yearly for the first five acres; $10.00 per year for areas between five and twenty-five acres, and $25.00 per year for areas between twenty-five and eighty acres. Permittees have exclusive possession of the permit areas.

Application for fur-farm lease on land outside the national forests must be made to the district land office in which the land is situated. Leases for fur-farming purposes on such lands may be issued for periods not exceeding ten years. Not more than 640 acres may be included in any such lease, unless the land applied for is an island, in which case the lease, within the discretion of the Secretary of the Interior, may be for an area not to exceed thirty square miles. Each lessee is required to pay a royalty of 1 per cent on the gross returns derived from the sale of live animals and pelts. However, each lessee must pay a minimum annual rental of $25 if the area of the tract leased does not exceed 640 acres, and a minimum annual rental of $50 if the area is more than 640 acres, if the 1-per-cent royalty does not equal or exceed such amounts.

The prospective fur farmer will get much encouragement from the Alaska Game Commission and other interested departments of the government, and leases are available on suitable tracts of land. Whole islands in the Aleutians are some-times leased, and here the breeding stock is permitted to run wild. These animals feed themselves on aquatic foods washed up on the beaches, until their numbers outgrow the available food. When the pelting season arrives, some of the animals are taken in enclosures surrounding their usual feeding ground; some are snared or trapped in the usual manner of taking wild animals.

It is suggested that those interested in fur farming in Alaska get in touch with the Alaska Game Commission, in Juneau, for information concerning fur farms for sale. Here, as in other industries, some that have tried it have not had the experience or other qualifications necessary for success, and fully or partially equipped farms, sometimes complete with breeding stock, are available. Other fur farms in suitable areas have been abandoned, and such leases with some abandoned improvements may be had. It would be wise, as in the case of agriculture, for the prospective fur farmer to come to Alaska and make a careful survey of the situation before he makes a permanent move or brings his family to Alaska. Invest-ment required depends so much upon the individual, and upon the extent of the fur farm and equipment, that an estimate is impractical.

The distribution of wild fur bearers throughout Alaska is roughly as follows:

Black bears in great numbers are found throughout most of the Territory, except the Arctic regions, the Alaska Peninsula, and the Aleutian chain, and Baranof, Admiralty, and Chichagof Islands of southeastern Alaska. However, their hides are of little commercial value. Brown and grizzly bears are classed as game animals, and the sale of any part thereof is prohibited.

Although polar bears are classed as fur animals, only about sixty-five skins are exported each year. Their range is on the Arctic coast, where the Eskimos use their flesh for food and their hides for various purposes. A painful but effective manner of taking polar bears was said to have been employed by the Eskimo prior to the advent of the high-powered rifle. Whalebone—of which the old-time corset stays were made— was rolled into a tight ball. This ball was in turn enclosed in a piece of putrid seal blubber and placed where the bear would find it. The hungry bear would gulp down the blubber, whalebone and all, and when digestion began to take place, the resilient whalebone stays would be released and fly outward, and the sharpened ends would pierce the bear's stomach and vitals and cause death.

Wolves range throughout the mainland, southeastern Alaska, and the Alaska Peninsula. They are especially numerous in the ranges of caribou and deer, and their depredations against the domestic reindeer herds are causing huge animal losses. Coyotes have only within the last decade found their way across the Canadian border into Alaska, and although their numbers are not yet sufficient to cause great damage, their potential increase is viewed with alarm. Wolves and coyotes are hunted for both bounty and hides, the pelts having sufficient value to return about $14,000 annually to trappers and hunters.

Mink, the most valuable of all Alaska's land fur bearers, is distributed widely throughout the Territory, except in the Arctic regions and along the Aleutian Island chain.

Red fox is distributed throughout nearly all of Alaska except the southeastern portion; blue fox, along the southern and southwestern shores, and especially the islands to the westward; white fox, along the northwest coast and adjacent islands. The five color varieties of foxes together—red, cross, silver, blue, and white—produce almost as much revenue as all other fur animals combined. The red fox produces cross variants in the ratio of about one to eight, and silvers about one to twenty.

Beavers are found along the streams of central and south central Alaska, almost to the western coast, and in limited numbers in southeastern Alaska.

Muskrats are the most abundant of Alaska fur bearers, producing an annual crop of more than 250,000 pelts. Wherever deltas are formed, muskrats are found. The shores of the Kobuk, Koyukok, Tanana, Copper, Kuskokwim, and Yukon Rivers teem with these little fur bearers. Although occasional severe winters that freeze ponds to the bottom bring about periods of scarcity, the muskrat crop is on the whole very steady.

Wolverine and lynx are distributed rather sparsely throughout the Territory, except in the extreme western mainland and westward islands.

Marten, or sable, and land otter inhabit central and southeastern Alaska, and otter range from the southeastern seacoast to the Arctic Circle. The otter has never been plentiful in Alaska, and the marten has become so scarce over most of its range that frequent closed seasons are necessary.

Of all the fur animals in Alaska, the weasel, source of the fur known as ermine, is perhaps the only fur bearer numerous in every part of Alaska, extending as far westward as Unimak Island. But the gathering of their little white pelts is of relatively minor importance in the fur economy of the Territory. The annual catch of about twelve thousand pelts has remained unchanged for many years.

Aside from seals and sea otters, which, because of the rigid regulations on the take of the former and the strict closed season on the latter, are of only academic interest to the Alaska trapper at present, this describes the general distribution of fur-bearing animals.

It is apparent that further development of the fur industry in Alaska will be in the field of fur farming to a great extent. Yet there is considerable room in isolated districts of the north country for experienced trappers, especially those who are expert wolf trappers.

For one that loves the out-of-doors and has sufficient knowledge of Arctic conditions, the free—but by no means easy—life of the Alaska trapper offers a reasonable income in return for his efforts.

CHAPTER SEVEN

Prospecting and Mining

GOLD! A magic word that sets men's blood afire! The word that sent farmers, businessmen, professional men, bookkeepers, gamblers, adventurers—yes, and adventuresses too—into the cold of the Arctic, across snow-capped mountains, over precipitous trails where one slip meant oblivion and there were many slips. Some found gold and fortune; others, disappointment and disillusionment; and still others, indescribable suffering and untimely death.

The stories of romance and tragedy of the Klondike and Nome gold rushes, near the turn of the century, have been told innumerable times and still appear in current magazines. So, also, the stories of the dance-hall girls. Although these fabulous tales have ceased, for the most part, to come out of the north, the flow of gold has never ceased. From Alaska's gold mines have come half a billion dollars during the past half century, and it is estimated that much more gold remains in the Territory than has yet been taken out.

Gold is by no means the only metal that comes from Alaska mines. Copper, silver, platinum, tungsten, lead, tin, and other minerals—another half-billion dollars' worth—have been taken from Alaska mines, and the surface has barely been scratched.

It is a far cry from the old-time prospector with his pan and rocker to the skilled mineralogist with his stock of chemicals and supplies and the efficient hydraulic equipment capable of handling more ore in a day than the old prospector could handle in a season. But strangely enough, both systems survive to this day. And while it is true that the hardy old-timers are rapidly leaving this world and the younger generation is not taking up where the old left off, still the lure of gold and the life of a prospector have much that is attractive to a man that enjoys the simple outdoor life. Rugged individuals that are willing to gamble at long odds for high stakes have been known to discover one commercial mineral deposit that has resulted in its owner's becoming financially independent for life. However, a person that is unwilling to accept hardships and disappointments should choose some occupation other than prospecting.

Some discoveries are pure luck, but by far the greater number are the results of careful surveys by educated and experienced geologists or thorough prospecting by experienced prospectors. Instances have been known where geologists have passed up certain areas that later produced fabulous mines when some experienced prospector kept puttering about and refused to accept the conclusion of the geologist. The Premier mine near Hyder is said to be just such a discovery. Sometimes a whole group of geologists brand an area as nonproductive, and another geologist refuses to accept their findings and makes an important discovery. This happened recently in the Yellowknife Mining Area of Yukon Territory, and now the whole district is a beehive of activity.

However, the time has definitely passed when a prospector can afford to go into the field with a working knowledge of gold only. He might pass up a fortune in other valuable metals or minerals. And there is little excuse today for lack of knowledge on the part of the prospector. Short courses in mining are being conducted by the University of Alaska at Ladd Field near Fairbanks, Fort Richardson, Seward, Juneau, Ketchikan, Sitka, Metlakatla, Anchorage, and Haines. Interested persons should write the University of Alaska, College, Alaska. The University also publishes a very complete book, *Determinative Mineralogy for the Alaskan Prospector*, price one dollar plus fifteen cents postage. This book gives a list of the twenty-one items of equipment necessary to test seventy-five minerals mentioned in the book, and a most complete and simply worded description of how each sample may be identified. If the prospector will take the short course, which gives him actual experience in testing the various minerals likely to be encountered in Alaska and elsewhere in North America, then supply himself with the suggested equipment and a copy of the book with which to refresh his memory, he will be equipped to take full advantage of his prospecting work.

The University of Washington also offers a prospector's course, open without examination to all men past high school age. The course includes testing of ores as well as field work, and requires ninety days or longer to complete. Application may be made to the University of Washington, Mines Laboratory, Seattle 5, Washington.

For the benefit of those that may, in connection with other outside work, happen upon specimens that they think may be valuable, and so that the prospector may substantiate his own findings, fully equipped assay offices of the Territorial Department of Mines are maintained in Juneau, Ketchikan, Anchorage, and College (Fairbanks). Prospectors are encouraged to submit samples to the most convenient office. When possible to do so, carefully taken channel samples should be submitted rather than hand-picked samples. Ofttimes, with the knowledge of rock or possibly qualitative tests, exhaustive assaying work is unnecessary. A brief description of the approximate location, which is kept strictly confidential, is of assistance to the assayer and is helpful to the department in maintaining proper files on mineral resources.

Field engineers in the employ of the Department of Mines are available for examining prospects, if the owner is unable to employ a private engineer. Services include mapping, and making available necessary data to submit to financiers and others for the purpose of securing financial assistance in developing the discovery or for sale of the property. Requests for such assistance should be addressed to the Commissioner of Mines, Juneau, Alaska.

Equipment for sawing and polishing stone is a part of the facilities of the Territorial Department of Mines at College. Rock or minerals suspected of being useful as ornamental stones or gems may be sent to that office, where a polished surface will be prepared and returned to the sender with a report of its possible usefulness and value.

The collection and sale of specimen material and gem stones, both semiprecious and precious, is fast becoming an important item in connection with Alaska prospecting. Jade, for which China is famous, is now being mined commercially in the vicinity of the Kobuk River near Shungnak 150 miles east of Kotzebue on Alaska's northwestern coast. Garnet, ruby, sapphire, topaz, turquoise, and tourmaline are likewise possibilities of the Territory.

A very large proportion of Alaska has not been adequately prospected, and many parts of the Territory are without complete geologic maps or surveys, and some of the available maps are fifty years old. Here again is evidence of inadequate financing by the federal government in the matter of maintaining and developing Alaska's resources. Lack of funds for salaries comparable to those of private enterprise, and for expenses, has resulted in the recent loss of skilled personnel from the staff of the Commissioner of Mines, and years of training for new engineers, not familiar with Alaska and its mining problems, are necessary before they can attain the efficiency of the lost employees.

Even with this handicap, too much cannot be said about the excellent work of the office of the Commissioner of Mines and the results obtained; and Alaska is indeed fortunate to have a man at the head of that department so well fitted for the job and so vitally interested personally in his work that he fairly beams his enthusiasm. This man is Mr. B. D. Stewart. Many exceedingly informative pamphlets are published by his department, and two especially are recommended to anyone interested in prospecting in Alaska. One is *Prospecting in Alaska* by R. L. Stewart; the other i: *Industrial Minerals as a Field for Prospecting in Alaska* by A. E. Glover; and they may be obtained by addressing B. D. Stewart, Commissioner of Mines, Juneau, Alaska.

Mr. Stewart welcomes inquiry concerning prospecting, especially from ex-servicemen, and will gladly answer such inquiries. A great deal of the information in this chapter concerning prospecting areas for metals and minerals is condensed from the above bulletins, from other pamphlets from his office, and from personal conversation with Mr. Stewart.

A straight line drawn from the extreme tip of southeastern Alaska northwest to Nome bisects the principal known metallic mineral-deposit areas, which extend some two hundred miles on either side of such a line. Mineral springs are found along this same mineral-deposit area and also extend into southern and southwestern Alaska.

For the convenience of those that are considering prospecting in Alaska, a list of the different districts in Alaska with their known occurrences of minerals and metals, also prospects, climate, and accessibility is given herewith.

Southeastern Alaska: This is a rough mountainous country, heavily timbered and with heavy rainfall. The summers are cool and the winters average about 32 above zero. It is very difficult to penetrate except by boat along the coast and by float plane to inland lakes.

The Ketchikan area has produced copper, gold, silver, palladium, platinum, marble, and limestone, and it is also known to contain lead, zinc, chromium, iron, antimony, and molybdenum. Prince of Wales Island is a potential source of iron ore. This whole area is well mineralized, and it seems likely that additional discoveries will be made.

The Hyder district contains deposits of silver, lead, gold, copper, and tungsten ores. A small amount of gold has been produced, and ore containing scheelite has been mined and shipped. Ice and snow fields prevail in the higher mountains.

The Wrangell district has produced gold and garnets. Occurrences of zinc, silver, lead, pyrite, barite, graphite, marble, limestone, and fluorite are known to exist. The district probably deserves more attention from prospectors than has heretofore been accorded it.

The near-by Petersburg area has not been intensively prospected. Discoveries of lead, zinc, silver, gold, copper, chromite, manganese, barite, witherite, and coal have been reported, but there is no production as yet.

The Sitka district includes Baranof and Chichagof Islands.

Gold and silver to the value of around $20,000,000 have been produced on Chichagof Island, and there has been some production of gypsum. Baranof has had considerable gold-lode development but little production to date. Scheelite occurs on Lisianski Inlet. There are also large copper-nickel deposits in the district. Most of the beaches of the area have been cursorily examined, but much of the interior of the islands remains practically unexplored and is difficult of access.

The Juneau area, known as the Juneau Gold Belt, has produced gold, silver, and lead valued at approximately $150,-000,000. Other metals known to exist in the district are zinc, copper, antimony, nickel, molybdenite, manganese, iron, coal, and tremolite asbestos. More prospecting has been done in this district than in most sections of Alaska. However, the chances for additional discoveries in the almost inaccessible back country are considered good. The Glacier Bay National Monument has recently been thrown open to prospecting, and some sections of it are known to be well mineralized.

The Skagway precinct, including the Porcupine placer district has produced over $1,000,000 in gold. Little prospecting for lodes has been done in this vicinity although ledges carrying low values in gold, silver, lead, and copper are known to occur. Some development work has been done on deposits containing zinc, lead, and silver near Skagway. High-grade specimens of quartz containing gold and bornite from the Chilkat Valley area have been brought into Haines. Molybdenite occurs north of Skagway, and there is a magnetite occurrence in the vicinity of Haines.

South Central Coastal Region: The coastal region, reaching from Cape Spencer to the mouth of Cooper River, is heavily timbered and difficult of access, with precipitous mountains extending almost to the sea. Transportation is by boat, and by float plane to inland lakes. The climate is comparable to that of southeastern Alaska, but with somewhat less precipitation along the coast. In the Lituya Bay area small-scale placer mining along the beaches has been carried on with a total production of gold amounting to not more than $100,-000. The beaches as yet have not been thoroughly prospected, and little prospecting for lodes has been done in the vicinity, owing in part to its inaccessibility.

In the adjacent Yakutat Bay area similar placer operations have been carried on with small production. This area contains some small beds of lignitic coal, and copper mineralization has been noted.

A few miners earn a living by working the beaches near Yakataga, supplemented by fishing in season. There are several known petroleum seepages in the near-by mountains, and coal also occurs.

The important known mineral resources of the Controller Bay region are coal and petroleum. From the Katalla Oil Field in this district has come the only Alaska production of oil in commercial quantity. The district as a whole has not been thoroughly explored.

The Bering River field contains extensive beds of high-grade coal, undeveloped as yet on account of the lack of transportation, but a potential reserve when iron and steel development comes to the Pacific Coast.

Copper River Region: This area covers a large section, with corresponding variations in climate and rainfall from the heavy precipitation and mild climate of the coastal area to the comparatively dry, extremely cold inland district. Snow and ice cover parts of the mountainous sections in winter, and the district is laced with swift-flowing glacial streams, treacherous and difficult to cross. The upper portion of the area may be reached by way of a branch of the Richardson Highway to the Chitina district. Float planes can fly to inland lakes. Some gold-lode development has been carried on for a number of years between Cordova and the mouth of Copper River in the McKinley Lake area. Likewise, some placer production has come from the Bremner River area, and some promising gold lodes have been under development. Nickel-bearing lodes are known to occur near the head of Canyon Creek.

The Kennecott or Nizina district has produced over $200,-000,000 in copper, but the known deposits were worked out and abandoned in 1938. Much of the silver produced in Alaska has been a by-product of these copper operations. This district also produces placer gold and native copper. Some lode gold has been produced. The district as a whole is well mineralized, and it seems probable that additional commercial mineral deposits will be found.

Some placer mining has occurred in the upper White River district, also in the Chistochina district. Some platinum is associated with the placer gold in this area. The bedrock source of neither of these minerals has been found. Placer gold is widely distributed in the Nelchina district, which has recently been rendered more accessible by the Glenn Highway.

Prince William Sound: This area includes many islands, inlets or fiords, and bays. It is difficult of access, precipitation is heavy; the winters are mild with zero seldom recorded, and the summers are cool.

Extensive copper deposits occur in the Ellamar district, and other minerals include silver, lead, zinc, and iron. Some gold likewise occurs but has not proved of economic importance. The Valdez district has been an important producer of lode gold. Silver, lead, and copper are present in some of the ore. Small gold-bearing veins also occur in the near-by Tiekel district, but high transportation costs have prevented production. Silver, lead, and copper are also found. Some development of gold, silver, lead, zinc, and copper has occurred in the Unakwik Inlet area. A number of gold lodes have been located in the Port Wells area, and silver, lead, zinc, and copper are associated with the gold. Small veins carrying good values in gold and some silver, lead, zinc, and copper have recently been located in the Passage Canal area. A small vein in the Jackpot Bay area, discovered some years ago, was assayed at 2.5 ounces of gold per ton, and also contained silver, lead, and zinc.

Extensive copper deposits have been developed on Knight and Latouche Islands, and most of the copper from the region was produced by Kennecott Copper Corporation on Latouche.

Alaska Railroad Region: The terrain varies from high mountains to level muskeg, and the temperature in winter grows progressively colder with distance from the sea. Precipitation is moderate to light. More investigation of mineral resources has occurred in this region than in any other part of Alaska. A complete report, including geological maps—Bulletin No. 907, *Geology of the Alaska Railroad Region*—may be obtained at a price of $1.25 from the Superintendent of Documents, Washington 25, D.C.

Considerable high-grade chromite ore has been mined on the southern end of Kenai Peninsula. The western part of the peninsula is underlain by extensive beds of lignite coal. A small amount of gold also has been mined from beach placers of the west coast. At Nuka Bay, on the southeast coast of the peninsula, a number of gold lodes, some of which are comparatively high grade, have been developed. There also is some placer mining north of Seward.

Extensive beds of high-grade coal occur in the upper Matanuska Valley, and operating mines supply the lower rail belt and the Alaska Railroad with coal. A tremendous new discovery, estimated to contain 3,000,000 minable tons of high-grade coal, was recently reported from that district. The Willow Creek district is an important producer of lode gold. The Yentna or Cache Creek district is one of the most important gold placer camps of the Territory, and also furnishes some coal for local consumption. Gold development is under way in the Broad Pass district, and the Chulitna River area has lodes carrying gold, silver, lead, and zinc. There are numerous deposits of coal in the district.

Many farms in this Alaska Railroad region have their own private surface coal supply.

Placer gold has been mined for a number of years in the Valdez Creek district, and some promising gold lodes have been discovered. The Bonnifield region has long been an important placer gold camp, and gold, silver, and lead lodes have been developed to some extent. Placer gold has been mined in the Kantishna district, and lodes have yielded silver, lead, gold, and antimony.

The Healy River coal field produces coal for domestic use and for generation of power for the northern part of the rail belt.

The Fairbanks district is well named the "Golden Heart" of Alaska, as it is the principal producer of placer gold in the Territory. Scarcely a creek bed has escaped dredging, which has left rows of upturned rock and soil altogether as though a giant mole had burrowed underneath. The Fairbanks area has also produced substantial amounts of lode gold and some antimony and tungsten ore.

Southwestern Alaska: Climatic conditions are not severe except in the northern part. Rainfall varies from twenty to one hundred inches. Fog is common in the vicinity of the Alaska Peninsula and the Aleutians. The region is fairly accessible, but there are some sections that are difficult of access. No productive mining has been carried on in southwestern Alaska for a number of years, except small-scale beach operations on Kodiak Island. The region has not been extensively prospected although some sections are known to be well mineralized.

The Aleutian Islands have not been mapped geologically, and little is known of their mineral resources. Some high-grade zinc ore is known to occur on Sedanka and Unalaska Islands. Sulphur occurs on Akun Island and in other vicinities near volcanoes. Unga Island produced several million dollars in gold some fifty years ago. The ore also contained lead, silver, zinc, and copper. Some of these deposits might be worthy of additional investigation in view of improved methods of mining and milling. Coal also occurs on Unga. Popof Island has produced some beach placer gold, and there has been some development work on lodes in the vicinity. Some high-grade bituminous coal was mined at Herendeen Bay in the early days, and Chignik Bay as well as scattered localities of the Alaska Peninsula have coal deposits. Undeveloped gold, copper, and zinc prospects have been reported at Balboa Bay. Petroleum seepages have been found along the southern shore of the Alaska Peninsula, but no productive development has resulted from the few exploratory wells drilled there. Pumice occurs in the Valley of Ten Thousand Smokes and other places near volcanoes. Some silver was mined about thirty years ago near Cape Kubugakli. High-grade copper float has been found near Cape Douglas.

Some gold placer mining has been carried on for forty years along the beaches of the west coast of Kodiak Island. A small amount of platinum also has been recovered. Some development of gold lodes has been started, but no production of consequence is reported. Other minerals contained in the lodes include copper, zinc, lead, and silver, and the presence of tin in at least one of the lodes has been reported but not verified.

The Iliamna Lake vicinity has some promising copper lodes, from which a few tons of high-grade ore have been shipped. Prospecting in the area might possibly reveal hitherto undiscovered bodies. A small amount of placer gold has been mined on streams that flow into Lake Clark and Iliamna Lake.

Cinnabar has recently been discovered on Wood River in the Bristol Bay area. Some production of placer gold has come from the upper Mulchatna River. The headwaters of the Nushagak and its tributaries, and the region over the divide into the Kuskokwim drainage, have not been thoroughly prospected.

Kuskokwim River Region: The climate along the bay is comparatively mild, but the district in the interior is subject to sub-arctic temperatures. Winds and fog along the coast create more discomfort than the interior cold. Precipitation is light throughout most of the area. In summer, river steamers are available to McGrath. Landing fields are located at strategic points throughout the district, and the airplane is a favored mode of travel.

Since discovery of platinum in 1926 in the Goodnews Bay area, that district has become the principal producer of platinum metals in the United States and possessions. For many years placer gold has been mined on a small scale. More recent development in the Goodnews-Arolic region has increased this production considerably. Placer gold also occurs in varying amounts in the gravels of the upper Togiak, Kanektok, and Eek Rivers.

For several years the Tuluksak-Aniak region has contributed substantially to the gold output of the Territory, by large-scale placer mining operations. A large, unmapped, and only superficially prospected area extends from the Stony River southward in the general direction of Goodnews Bay across the Hoholitna, Holitna, and upper Aniak Rivers. It is probable that the area is worthy of a great deal more prospecting than has been done.

Cinnabar lodes occur in the vicinity of the old village of Kolmakof, near Sleitmut, and at the head of Crooked Creek south of Flat. There is some production in recent years, and stibnite accompanies the cinnabar in most of the deposits. The possibilities of discovering additional commercial bodies of cinnabar and of placer gold in the vicinity of the intrusives in this general area are said to have been by no means exhausted.

A lode deposit of gold-bearing antimony and others containing copper, gold, and silver occur in the Russian Mountains; however, no production has been recorded.

The gold placers of the Georgetown, Takotna, McGrath, and Nixon Fork districts have been steady producers for a period of years. Likewise the lodes of the Nixon Fork district. Most of the ore contains some copper.

Yukon Basin: This area contains the most important known placer deposits in the Territory, and approximately $200,-000,000 in gold has been mined in the area. The climate is semiarid and cold in winter, but not much colder than some areas in the States. Transportation is by river steamer in the summer, and by airplane, as landing fields are located at various settlements in the district. The lowland coastal area between the mouths of the Kuskokwim and Yukon Rivers has not been geologically mapped, and little is known of its mineral resources.

Some placer gold production occurred in the vicinity of Marshall about twenty-five years ago. Intensive prospecting might reveal the presence of other low-grade deposits. So far as is known very little attention has been given to a search for the lode source of the placer gold. Coal has been mined for local use in several near-by localities.

The Kaiyuh Hills have not been thoroughly prospected. Some placer gold and a small amount of silver-lead ore have been mined, but transportation difficulties prevented profitable operations. Geological conditions are said to indicate the possible presence of mineral deposits other than those heretofore discovered.

The Iditarod, Innoko, and Ruby districts have been highly productive of placer gold for many years. Some high-grade gold veins, with associated antimony, copper, lead, zinc, and tungsten, likewise occur. Other small veins containing gold, stibnite, and cinnabar occur in the district. One of the cinnabar lodes has produced some mercury. There has been some development in the Ruby district of silver-lead prospects, and some of the placers contain appreciable amounts of tin. The bedrock source of the tin-bearing material has not been discovered. Coal also occurs in the Iditarod area. More intensive prospecting for lodes will likely follow the depletion of the valuable placers in these well-mineralized districts.

The upper Koyukuk region in the vicinity of Wiseman has been a continuous producer of placer gold, most of it by the old hand method. So far, little attention has been given to lode prospecting. Geologic conditions appear to be favorable in the region.

The Chandalar district also has produced considerable placer gold, and some production from lodes has occurred. The country east of the Chandalar to the boundary has been prospected very little.

Placer gold is said to have been panned along the Coleen River, also a few miles east of the boundary at the heads of streams flowing into the Arctic Ocean. This suggests that the little-known area across the heads of the Coleen, Old Crow, and Firth might have possibilities for a placer camp. Prospecting in this area should be undertaken only by one familiar with the Arctic and well equipped to meet arctic conditions. Here a combination of trapping and prospecting is worthy of consideration.

The Yukon-Tanana region of about 38,000 square miles has been and is the principal placer-gold-producing area in Alaska. In addition to gold and silver, tin, tungsten, and antimony have been produced in the region on a commercial scale, and coal has been mined for local use. Deposits of lead, zinc, copper, chromium, iron, cobalt, nickel, platinum, molybdenum, and bismuth are known to be present. The southeastern portion of the region will be accessible by the Alaska

Highway. Other portions are now accessible by highway, river boats, and planes. The district is well described in U.S. Geological Survey Bulletin No. 872, *The Yukon-Tanana Region,* copies of which can be obtained at a price of seventy cents each from the Superintendent of Documents, Washington 25, D.C. Particular attention is called to suggestions for prospecting by the author that begin on page 264 of that bulletin.

The Chisana and Nabesna areas, south of the upper Tanana region, have produced some placer and lode gold. Copper also is available in commercial quantities except for the difficulties of transportation.

Northwestern Alaska: Much of this area lies above the Arctic Circle, where arctic conditions must be met. The coastal area is approachable by steamship in summer, and the rest of the district is served by landing fields, and experienced pilots often land ski-equipped planes on the snow wherever flat surfaces of sufficient size can be found.

The area between the mouth of the Yukon and Norton Bay has not been mapped. Bonanza Creek produced some gold in the early days, and large-scale operations have been carried on in recent years.

Seward Peninsula is second only to the Yukon-Tanana region in the production of placer gold. Everybody is familiar with the history of the Nome area of gold-rush days, and no further discussion of that district is necessary, except that today large-scale methods are employed on lower-grade ground and account for a major portion of the production in the district. In spite of the fact that some areas on the peninsula have been intensively prospected and mined over a long period, there are said to be several sections that have not yet been thoroughly prospected and that are considered to be favorable. Some placer tin has been mined, and lodes have been discovered, but little lode production has resulted. Other minerals found in lodes on the peninsula include gold, silver, lead, bismuth, antimony, tungsten, copper, iron, mercury, platinum, and coal.

Very little prospecting has been done on St. Lawrence Island, as this district is a reserve and not open for location under the mining laws. There are known occurrences of molybdenum, copper, iron, lead, silver, and tin on the island, and quartz containing high values in gold has also been discovered.

A large unmapped and practically unprospected mountainous area lies between Kobuk and Noatak rivers. Although the region is known to be well mineralized and is probably the most favorable area in the Territory for new discoveries of commercial deposits, little prospecting has been done. Transportation has hindered development of known mineralized areas of the upper Kobuk, Noatak, and Alatna rivers. Prospectors interested in this region should be well financed and equipped and should avail themselves of the quickest means of transportation in order that the maximum amount of time may be spent in search for minerals. Little effort has been made to locate or develop lodes, although favorable indications have been noted in several localities. Copper, lead, silver, iron, coal, jade, asbestos, and quartz crystals occur in the district, and specimens containing columbite and tantalite have been obtained north of Kiana.

Northern Alaska: Arctic conditions exist in this area. Precipitation is light. Transportation is by steamer during the summer and by airplane in winter. The Arctic slope as far

A homestead near Anchorage. (*Copyright Jack Maycock*)

The farmer in Alaska can rear his family in the clean environment of the outdoors, where wholesome recreation is at hand the year round. (*Copyright The Alaska Sportsman*)

Alaska is famous for the quality and size of its vegetables, especially root crops. (*Copyright Forest Service*)

Cool, damp summers, long days, and fertility of Alaska soil combine to produce bountifully. (*Copyright Forest Service*)

Although the growing season is short in the Tanana Valley near Fairbanks, the long hours of daylight in summer produce excellent grain crops. (*Copyright Harry T. Becker*)

A strawberry patch in Alaska. Many kinds of berries produce abundantly throughout the Territory. (*Copyright Forest Service*)

Some valleys in Alaska provide excellent pasturage, such as this homesite in Eagle River Landing. There are many fine dairies throughout Southeastern Alaska. (*Copyright Forest Service*)

A Matanuska Valley farm. Mr. and Mrs. Paul Nelson and their
flock of white leghorns.

east as the lower Colville River has long been a naval petroleum reserve and not subject to location. This reserve has recently been extended to include the remaining part of the slope. Extensive beds of coal, some of which is high grade, are widely distributed in this section of the Territory.

Oil deposits in this region are now being developed by the Navy. However, the work has recently been turned over to private contractors, who will be supplied with all the data accumulated by the Navy relative to geologic formations and proper equipment, together with a detailed report on all operations to date. Oil oozing from the ground in this area is said to be the highest test of any known field. It accumulates in depressions and forms lakes of considerable size. Ducks which alight on these pools, mistaking them for water, get oil in their feathers and are unable to fly. Surveys indicate that within this district lies one of the largest untapped oil fields in North America.

Very little prospecting has been done in this section, although placer gold prospects are said to have been panned in the streams of the eastern part, notably the Okpilak River. Prospects of gold and other minerals are also reported to have been found on the north slopes of the Endicott Mountains.

If a prospector makes a discovery in Alaska, it is a relatively simple matter to perfect a claim. For either lode or placer claim, the locator must erect at each corner or angle of the claim posts of wood or monuments of stone not less than three feet in height nor less than three inches in diameter, showing the name of the claim, position or number of the monument, and the direction of the boundary lines; and the boundary lines must be cut out, blazed, or otherwise marked to make sure they may be easily traced. He must also post on the surface at or near the point of discovery, a plain sign or notice containing the name or number of the claim, the name of locator or locators, the date of location, and the number of feet in length and breadth on each side of the vein, if a lode claim.

He must within ninety days record the claim with the recorder of the recording district in which the claim is located, showing the name or number of the claim; length and width, in feet, of claim; dates of discovery and of posting notice of location, name of locator or locators, and a description of the claim with reference to some natural object or permanent monument, so that an intelligent person could identify it.

He must within ninety days after the first of July of each year, until patent is issued therefor, file an affidavit that he has performed, individually or by paid labor, not less than a hundred dollars' worth of labor on his claim.

Under a recent court decision, it appears that a claim holder of a mine in Alaska, although he has not complied with the requirement that he do the hundred dollars a year assessment work, may resume work on the mine and retain ownership, if in the meantime it has not been relocated by someone else.

His placer claim must not cover more than twenty acres, and unless narrowed down because of claims alongside, must not be more than 1,320 feet long, and with the area limited to twenty acres this automatically limits the width to 660 feet. He cannot file more than two claims a month in the same recording district.

However, two additional placer claims may also be located in each month on behalf of each of two other persons whose powers of attorney are held by the locator, provided such powers of attorney have previously been recorded in the mining precinct where the locations are made.

The maximum size of a lode claim is 1,500 by 600 feet. There is no limit to the number of lode claims that may be located. No specific years of annual labor are required before patent can be issued. The requirement is that five hundred dollars' worth of improvements must be placed on each claim before patent can be applied for.

Copies of the Territorial laws governing the location and holding of mining claims may be obtained from the office of the Commissioner of Mines at Juneau. A prospector should through inquiry learn the location of the recording office for the precinct within which he expects to work. It is impractical to publish a map showing the forty-seven precincts, as the boundaries are changed often.

Coal lands are subject to permit and lease from the Secretary of the Interior on a royalty and rental basis. Leases may be had on oil and gas lands. The maximum area that may be held under coal permit or lease is 2,560 acres. Provision is also made for the issuance by the General Land Office for free-use licenses on ten-acre tracts from which coal may be mined for the use of the licensee without payment of royalty.

Radioactive public mineral lands have been withdrawn from private control by executive order of September 13, 1945, except valid prior claims, and are not now subject to being filed upon or otherwise controlled by individuals.

From the foregoing report by districts throughout Alaska it may readily be seen that very little of Alaska has been adequately prospected and that great possibilities exist for one properly trained and equipped to cope with situations that arise in this rough and partially uncharted territory.

Many factors should be taken into account before the prospector embarks on a prospecting venture in Alaska. The history of the Territory is replete with accounts of discoveries of known commercial possibilities, but so inaccessible that they could not be successfully developed. First and foremost, therefore, is the consideration of ability to commercialize his find. In this connection the prospector should keep constantly abreast of highway construction and highway opening, as of the Alaska Highway, and other newly installed transportation facilities into heretofore inaccessible regions known to be highly mineralized.

Ordinary equipment and supplies for the prospector and miner may be purchased in Alaska in any of the larger towns and in many of the smaller towns and trading posts scattered throughout the Territory. The dealers through years of experience have learned to stock those items best suited to the district, and in most cases the prices are comparable to those of the Pacific Coast plus freight. Game and fish are available in many sections of Alaska to augment or vary the food supply of the prospector.

The amount of cash necessary is from a thousand dollars upward depending upon the distance from source of supply, length of time the prospector expects to spend on the trip, and so forth. Canada has a grubstake plan in effect which has proved its worth in that it has produced one or more new finds. In 1945 Canada grubstaked eighty prospectors, and one of them, D. C. "Charlie" Ault, is reported to have discovered a major vein of gold ore on Truax Mountain in the Bridge River district. The Mines Minister, E. C. Carson, is said to be highly pleased with the grubstaking plan. One such strike, if it pans out well, will more than repay the province for the entire expense of grubstaking the whole group of prospectors. And still another gold-silver prospect is at present being investigated. This discovery, like the Truax Mountain find, was made by a grubstaked prospector.

A similar plan has been introduced in the territorial legislature—H. B. 102—and all interested people seem to be in accord that such a plan should be adopted in Alaska.

It is the opinion of Commissioner B. D. Stewart and others that every possible encouragement should be given experienced and capable prospectors in Alaska. The head of a large commercial company said recently that what Alaska needs most in the mining field is more prospecting, that only a few men are going into the hills at present, and without it the mining of gold and other minerals and metals would eventually cease. He, like others, recommends that the Territory or the federal government have a grubstaking plan.

The nation's mineral resources are being rapidly depleted, according to a 1946 report of the Interior Department. There was at that time less than a year's supply of mercury and less than two years' supply of manganese. Lead would run out in twelve years, according to the report, silver in eleven years, zinc nineteen, and copper thirty-four, unless new deposits were discovered to offset the rapidly depleting supply. Nearly all of these items are known to exist in many parts of Alaska.

It should be repeated that Alaska offers excellent opportunities for the trained and equipped prospector, and much new mining development will be made profitable with the completion of proposed new highways.

CHAPTER EIGHT

Lumbering
and Associated Industries

THE lumber industry in Alaska has expanded in recent years, and many believe that lumber and its associated industries offer a solution to much of the development problem of Alaska. It is difficult to provide roads and other transportation facilities to support agricultural development, stock raising, and so forth, without a permanent population of sufficient size to absorb the increased output of the farms and ranches and to help pay for the upkeep of those roads. Lumber industries could easily supply a good share of that permanent population.

Present lumber development centers around sawmills employed in getting out lumber for local construction, piles, and lumber for fish traps, piers, and some high-grade spruce that is exported for airplane stock. Ketchikan, Juneau, and Whittier each have a sawmill with approximately 100,000 feet capacity, and Wrangell has a mill with a capacity of about 65,000 feet.

Considerable timber is used by settlers, miners, and residents for firewood and for construction of homes and related structures. They are permitted to take such timber from the national forests in Alaska for their personal use, free of charge. No permit is required except for green saw timber.

The afore-mentioned mills, a few cabinet shops in the larger towns, and use of lumber by individuals account for practically all the production from Alaska forests at present, and it is safe to say that the lumber taken out thus far can hardly be missed.

One of the most impressive sights in all Alaska, and truly a lumberman's dream, is to stand in a thickly wooded Alaska coastal forest and look up and down the ridges at the tremendous array of huge trees, or to gaze upward at the tall, straight boles of the trees, many of which are smooth and without limbs for a hundred feet or more.

The coastal forest region of 43,000 square miles produces western hemlock, Sitka spruce, red and Alaska cedar; the interior forested area of some 342,000 square miles contains white spruce, birch, and cottonwood. Western red cedar is found in the southern part of southeastern Alaska. This is excellent shingle material and is used extensively for cabinet-making. Alaska cedar is a beautiful wood, bright yellow in color, and is also widely used in cabinetmaking. It is used too for battery separators.

Western hemlock is the prevailing commercial type of wood along Alaska's coastal forests. It is hard enough to stand up well under heavy wear, and sufficiently soft to be worked easily. It is good for flooring, heavy timbers, and inside finish; and it is superior to eastern hemlock as a pulping wood. It is in demand for boxes and crates, and is used as piling for fish traps, and for ties.

Sitka spruce is the principal saw-timber tree of southeastern Alaska. It is used for all kinds of lumber as well as airplane stock. The lower grades are made into packing cases for the salmon industry. Exporting of high-grade spruce lumber for airplane stock started during World War I, and exports have increased every year. Sitka spruce is also an excellent pulping wood.

There are great possibilities for pulp mills in Alaska. Recently the government has spent large sums of money getting the timber cruised for this purpose; and many special inducements, such as long-time contracts, paying as cutting proceeds, and other first-come-first-served advantages, are expected to attract one or more large paper manufacturers to the Territory.

One offer of the government to induce private pulp manufacturers to Alaska is said to embrace some 14,000,000 cords (about 7,500,000,000 feet) of spruce and hemlock near Ketchikan for a sulphate, sulphite, or newsprint plant. This particular offer comes at a time when there is a shortage of pulpwood in the States and the available forest resources are constantly shrinking.

It is also said that many times that amount of suitable timber is available if the demand warrants.

On the estimate of the commercial stand of virgin timber of the Tongass National Forest and public domain of southeastern Alaska at eighty billion board feet, and with eighty years allowed as the rotation period during which this virgin timber may be removed entirely under sustained-yield forest management, approximately one million tons of newsprint (more than one fourth of the requirement of the United States) can be produced yearly without depletion of forests.

The postwar period offers a considerably increased demand for sulphate pulp, as newly developed refining and bleaching processes have resulted in many new uses for this type of pulp.

Favorable factors for the industry include water transportation for logs from the woods to the mills and for paper from the mills to market; low logging costs because of readily accessible timber (estimated at six dollars per hundred cubic feet for peeled pulpwood logs delivered at Alaska local mills); high volume per acre; and a climate which permits mill operations and shipping throughout the year. Three fourths of the timber is said to be within two and a half miles of tidewater.

The area in which the pulp timber covered by this offer is located has a system of navigable fiords. Near-by Prince Rupert, B.C., is the closest transcontinental railhead—approximately ninety-five miles from Ketchikan. Navigation to Prince Rupert is through the sheltered inland passage and is especially suitable for small motor-driven cabin boats and barge service, and large steamers ply this passage the year round.

An outline of the agreement provisions for sale of the pulptimber unit near Ketchikan appears at the end of this chapter. They are the general contract conditions for any proposed pulp sale in Alaska and were made public for study by interested people. More detailed contract conditions would have to be worked out for this and other timber units which might be offered for sale.

It will be noted by reference to this agreement that only the stumpage is offered for sale from the national forests, the land being retained by the United States for production of successive forest crops.

The government also encourages the establishment of additional sawmills to supply the local demand, especially those providing year-long operations and using efficient milling methods and first-class equipment. Minor woodworking industries, particularly those using western red and Alaska cedar, will be encouraged.

The recent stumpage price received for Sitka spruce, western red cedar, and Alaska cedar for sawmill use was $1.50 per thousand board feet; hemlock, $1.00; piling from 1¢ to

1½¢ per linear foot. Large units of pulp timber are expected to bring in the neighborhood of 60¢ per cord of a hundred cubic feet for spruce, and 40¢ for hemlock.

Because of the proximity of all Alaska timber to water, donkey engines and wire rope, similar to those in operation in Washington and Oregon, are the most practical means of moving logs. Floating logging camps are also widely used.

One special feature of the national forest timber area is the abundance of water power in units of suitable size for individual industrial plants. The best sites range from 5,000 to 30,000 horsepower in capacity and can be very economically developed for a year-round supply. A typical power site has a high "hanging lake" a short distance inland that provides excellent water storage facilities, and requires only short conduits to connect the lake with a powerhouse located at tidewater. All power sites are publicly owned and may be leased under the Federal Power Act for periods not exceeding fifty years.

One of the most promising groups of small industries awaiting development in Alaska is small woodworking plants making many items entering into house construction and turning out hundreds of wooden articles for everyday use. Alaska will consume increasing amounts of these things. It is recommended that skilled woodworkers or groups of such workers that have sufficient capital investigate these possibilities. In connection with such investigation it would be well to bear in mind that while the mills of southeastern Alaska can probably furnish all the spruce and hemlock required for such operations, any unusual demand for western red or Alaska cedar would require special arrangements for the logging of these species, and all species would require special logging to fill additional requirements in the interior.

Alaska has few small woodworking establishments at present,

and such articles must be shipped from the States. High costs of transportation will probably prohibit selling outside of Alaska, but these same high transportation costs act as a kind of tariff against incoming goods and give a certain amount of protection against outside competition for Alaska-made merchandise.

Manufacturing of furniture should offer excellent opportunities in Alaska. The demand is now greater than the available supply, and with the influx of many new settlers this demand should greatly increase in the next few years. Many types of furniture will be needed—serviceable but inexpensive furniture for the new settlers, high quality furniture for the town dwellers in the upper income brackets. For the first type, western hemlock, Alaska cedar, and Sitka spruce are available in southeastern Alaska, white spruce and Alaska white birch in the interior; for the higher quality, western and Alaska cedar in southeastern Alaska, birch in the interior. These species can be readily worked and finished into beautiful furniture. Birch veneer can also be used to cover other wood stock in Alaska, and produces beauty of grain and figure that cannot be otherwise obtained. Alaska cedar and western red cedar are excellent woods for closet linings and chests used for storing clothes, as both are insect and rodent repellents.

Alaska summer homes, maintained in the vicinity of nearly all towns in southeastern Alaska, afford a good market for locally designed furniture for porch and lawn use.

Sitka spruce is well suited for making breadboards, cutting boards, ironing boards, drainboards, stepladders, and other common household necessities. Alaska cedar and Alaska white birch make good turned articles such as table and floor lamps, candlesticks, mallets, bowls, toys, and picture frames. Rolling pins, plates, trays, salt and pepper shakers, and handles for files, shovels, and picks can be made from birch. Smoke stands, umbrella stands, hall trees, and stools can be made from nearly any species of Alaska wood.

A good market for well-worked logs for housebuilding will be found in all of the larger communities. Suppliers should be prepared to produce either hand-worked or sawed logs. Small mills could be used to face the logs on three sides, leaving the fourth side with the natural curve.

There will be an excellent and expanding market for western red cedar shingles for roofs and side walls. Plenty of material will be found along the shore line of the islands and the mainland of southeastern Alaska, but large production will likely necessitate special logging.

Until recent years over 90 per cent of roofing materials were imported from the States, and even now the greater proportion is imported. This seems inexcusable in view of the fact that western red cedar of Alaska is reputed to be the best shingle cedar on the coast, when clear, solid blocks are used, because of the narrow growth rings of the local trees. However, good cedar shingle material in Alaska logs is harder to secure, as defects, due to the far-northern range, are more common there than along Puget Sound.

Other cedar products, which are designed to use small blocks unsuited for shingle material, are net floats, decoy ducks, trays, dishes, boxes, and carving blocks.

The principal means of transportation throughout Alaska's maze of fiords, bays, and inlets is by boat. It is apparent to anyone familiar with the Territory that a well-equipped small boatbuilding business would flourish. Over two thousand seine and trolling boats and hundreds of pleasure craft ply the streams and waterways of Alaska, and many of these come from Puget Sound. The great majority of these boats are of heavy construction and are less than forty feet long.

There is a tremendous potential market for small craft in Alaska, and this industry should be especially promising. Expert craftsmen would do well to study the opportunities to establish small boat shops in the several Alaska ports. Alaska cedar would be the local timber most used for planking, decking, and numerous other purposes.

The logging and hewing of Alaska cedar knees could be developed into a small specialized enterprise, since knees from this species are preferred in ship and small boat construction. Commercial tests of Alaska cedar indicate that it is equal or perhaps superior to Douglas fir or Port Orford cedar, which are used in large quantities for this purpose on Puget Sound. Countless numbers of cedar knees which will produce the width required are obtainable in southeastern Alaska.

Skiffs are carried by every boat, and western red cedar is preferred for their construction because of its light weight, workability, and durability. Most of the skiffs used in Alaska waters should be produced locally.

Facilities for repairing small vessels are needed in every coastal town. Some of the towns already have marine ways, but others are entirely without. Chambers of commerce should be queried for most favorable locations.

Spruce oars are especially in demand, not only for Alaska boats but for export sale. Sitka spruce is unexcelled for oar material, and two small plants at Ketchikan have had to turn down large outside orders. Boat oar manufacturers could also produce pike poles, broom handles, gaff hook handles, and other similar turned articles.

Mild-cured and pickled fish require barrels or tierces, and Alaska's supply has largely been imported. Sitka spruce and western hemlock are considered good barrel material. Large boxes for shipping fresh and frozen fish are manufactured in the Territory, but the local supply is not sufficient for local needs.

Novelty and curio shops are operated in all of the principal towns throughout Alaska, and the sale of trinkets will be enlarged to meet the demands of visitors pouring into Alaska. While the demand for carved ivory, baskets, totem poles, and other items commonly supplied by the Indians and Eskimos is fairly well met locally, large quantities of other type novelties are obtained outside. Attractive and distinctive novelties from native woods would include ash trays, book ends, guest-book covers, trays, plates, spoons, paperweights, tie racks, carved figures of animals and birds, and many other objects. Popular animals to carve are bears, reindeer, mountain sheep, foxes, walrus, seals, whales, and sled dogs. Birds include eagles, ducks, ptarmigan, sea gulls, ravens, geese, and swans.

Novelty plants should be established near mills where the inexpensive scrap material of insufficient size for ordinary use may be obtained. The suitable woods of southeastern Alaska are Sitka spruce, western red cedar, and Alaska cedar. Birch is the outstanding species of interior Alaska for this purpose, but white spruce is also acceptable for numerous items.

Toys also could be manufactured in connection with novelties, and novelties of skins, such as coin purses, billfolds, comb cases, and so forth, could be included. In this connection, the recent experiments with sharkskin and the skins of sea mammals may produce excellent local substitutes for leather, and the skins of certain animals common to Alaska may also be used.

There is a potential market in Alaska for many thousands

of railroad ties, as approximately 50 per cent of the ties used before the war on the Alaska Railroad were imported.

In this category, float logs and piling and mining timbers are used in great quantities in Alaska. A large proportion of this type material was produced in Alaska before the war, but increased demand due to expanding industry will have to be met.

Wood preservation plants represent a greater investment than the minor wood-using industries. However, there is a good market for treated timber among the salmon canneries, mining companies; municipal, territorial, and government construction agencies, and other agencies that maintain waterfront structures. There is said to be enough work of this type on the coastal section of Alaska to supply continuous work for one 7-by-130-foot retort using creosote, and interior Alaska will provide 210 days' work per year for a 7-by-130-foot retort using creosote. The first initial plant should probably be installed at Whittier, Anchorage, or some point in southeastern Alaska where local mills could supply material. The more northerly plant should be somewhere on the Alaska Railroad and would have access to the new mill at Whittier. The most suitable material for such treatment is western hemlock.

There is some local market for poles for telephone, telegraph, and power lines, and it is possible that some market will develop in the States for western red cedar from Alaska, as pole-sized cedar has almost reached a vanishing point in the Pacific northwest. The vicinity of Ketchikan can furnish a good supply of such poles.

Definite opportunity exists in Alaska for small wood-products industries, and it is suggested that a modest beginning, expanding the plant as a market is created, would be the best policy.

Any discussion concerning lumber and its associated industries would not be complete without a brief word relative to the activity of the United States Forest Service in Alaska. In addition to supervising vast forested areas, they are constantly on the alert to avoid forest fires—Alaska's greatest destroyer of timber—and to bring them under control once they are started. They check all sawmill operations, scale lumber, set aside areas of timber for seeding purposes, set aside other areas within the national forests suitable for agriculture and make them available for homesteading; they reserve certain districts of special recreational value, build docks, trails, and bridges to make otherwise inaccessible regions easily accessible, and enter into various other activities too numerous to mention. The men in charge of the Alaska Region are sincerely interested in Alaska and every phase of the forest program—especially plans for sustained forest yield without depletion, so that posterity may enjoy the benefits and recreational advantages offered by Alaska's magnificent forests.

They print and distribute many fine pamphlets, and anyone interested in development of lumbering or associated industries should address an inquiry to the United States Department of Agriculture, Forest Service, Alaska Region, Juneau, Alaska, Mr. B. Frank Heintzleman, Regional Forester. A very complete booklet entitled *Opportunities for Minor Wood Product Industries in Alaska* by Alva W. Blackerby, Administrative Officer, is available from that office. A great deal of the information contained herein concerning minor wood-products opportunities is condensed from that booklet, and members of the Forest Service in the Alaska office contributed greatly to the information in this entire chapter.

Except for pulp and the few other forest products mentioned before, it is not believed advisable at this time to plan extended milling in Alaska with the thought of exporting. Because of the distance and high freight rates between the Territory and the States, and other factors of costs, it is not likely that the mill run of lumber from the predominating hemlock-spruce forests can compete with the materials of the same species produced in southern British Columbia, Washington, and Oregon. Lack of sufficient market for by-products is another drawback to processing for competitive export. The sawmill capacity in Alaska should be gauged to local demand, and if this is done the supply of high-grade saw timber will be sufficient to maintain a thriving lumber industry. With every town in southeastern Alaska—in fact, every town of any size in Alaska—planning a building program, local demand undoubtedly can consume a considerably increased production in future. Juneau's expansion plans are far advanced; likewise Ketchikan's. Anchorage has been in the process of a building boom for several years.

Anyone interested in establishing pulp manufacturing plants, sawmills, and wood-using industries should first come to Alaska and personally investigate the possibilities, then plan his operations in a manner that will conform to conditions existing within the Territory.

CONTRACT CONDITIONS FOR PROPOSED
PULP-TIMBER SALE IN ALASKA *

Timber contract will cover about 7,500,000,000 board feet, and is based on requirements for a 50-year supply of 150 tons

---

* This proposed contract covers a specific sale. Special conditions governing other pulp-timber sales will be worked out with prospective buyers.

daily for the first 10 years and 525 tons daily for the remaining 40 years.

Logging units within the sale area to be designated in advance for 5-year periods by the Forest Service.

The timber designated is not to be inferior to that commonly logged on the British Columbia coast.

The purchaser must agree to install a pulp mill of 150 tons' daily capacity within 3 years, and must increase the capacity to 525 tons within 10 years. Failure of the 10-year requirement will subject the contract to cancellation, and failure to meet the enlarged requirement will result in a reduction of the total timber volume to capacity.

The bid rates of the successful bidder will apply for the first 5-year period. Material regardless of species is to be scaled in units of 100 cubic feet of solid wood and will be paid for at one rate. Higher grades of Sitka spruce logs 24 inches and larger in top diameter will be scaled as saw logs and paid for at the saw-log rate. Provision is made for payment by board feet or linear feet for logs to be used for other purposes than pulp. Rates are based on 5-year periods subject to adjustment, but in no event are to be lower than originally appraised.

The original rate is to be based with consideration of competitive industries and the risk that will be a feature of the establishment of this enterprise in this new pulp-producing area.

Timber will be paid for as cutting proceeds, in installments of $10,000 to $40,000.

Two thirds of the purchaser's yearly pulpwood requirements are to be taken from the area under sale to him. The remainder may be taken outside. The minimum yearly amount to be taken from the purchaser's sale areas will be 5,000,000 cubic feet, maximum 31,500,000, but may be changed for any year with approval of the Forest Service.

Timber areas having special scenic value, such as those along narrow waterways of the main steamer routes, may be reserved from cutting.

Up to 10 per cent of the timber on any logging chance must be left for seeding purposes; this is subject to modification at reappraisal periods.

Trees with one or more logs 20 feet long and 12 inches in top diameter and having a net volume of not less than 25 per cent of the total volume of the tree will be cut.

All logs are merchantable which are 15 feet or longer, have a diameter of not less than 6 inches at the small end, and are at least 50 per cent sound.

Provision is made for utilization of extra high-grade timbers by manufacturers, also availability.

Purchaser must take adequate precaution against fires; the spawning of salmon must not be disturbed; local labor must be used if sufficiently skilled.

The agreement cannot be assigned without approval of the Forest Service Chief, but may be used as bond security.

Surety bond of $50,000 is required.

The sale is to be advertised, and sealed bids must be accompanied by required deposit of probably $100,000 to ensure compliance with contract. This deposit will be credited to his stumpage payments if he complies with contract.

CHAPTER NINE

Commercial Fishing

FOR many years commercial fishing has been Alaska's principal industry. The annual production is in excess of 500,000,000 pounds, valued wholesale at some $55,000,000. The fisheries employ approximately 25,000 persons and pay about 80 per cent of the annual territorial taxes.

During the summer fishing season nearly everybody along Alaska's coast line engages in some phase of the fishing industry. Many persons otherwise employed have arrangements with their employers that enable them to take advantage of the handsome returns enjoyed by those that fish commercially or work in processing plants during the short net and trap season of thirty to ninety days. Many own their own fishing gear and boats, while others fish for the canneries on a percentage basis. Some fish from tiny one-man gasoline boats, while others use elaborate boats with crews of as many as a dozen men. Income varies, of course, with prevailing price and the amount of the catch; however, it is not unusual for the individual fisherman to earn several thousand dollars in one season.

Importation of many thousands of workers from the States and the influx of many others from the interior crowd the fishing camps and near-by towns to overflowing. Transport planes bring needed workers from isolated sections in the north country, even Eskimos from as far away as Point Barrow, and return them when the season ends. A miniature stampede not unlike the gold-rush days occurs every year, and the streets of coast towns take on a holiday air.

The principal commercial fishes are salmon, sablefish, halibut, herring; clams, crabs, and shrimp; and miscellaneous fishes such as cod, rockfish, and flounder.

By far the most important food fish in Alaska is the salmon, of which there are five principal species: the Chinook or king, the silver or coho, the pink or humpback, the chum or dog, and the red, sockeye, or blueback.

All species of Pacific salmon migrate from the ocean to fresh water to spawn. The adult fish deposits the eggs in the nest, which is dug in the stream or lake bed, and the eggs are covered with gravel to a depth of several inches. The newly hatched fish are attached to the yolk sac for about a month, and during that time they live in the gravel nest and gradually absorb the yolk, which sustains them during the semi-larval stage. Then the young salmon wiggle up to the surface of the stream and forage for food the same as other minnows.

Both the eggs and the young fish are preyed upon constantly by other species of fish, which undoubtedly acted as nature's check on overproduction until the advent of man into the picture, which unbalanced it somewhat. For a time Alaska paid a bounty on Dolly Varden trout, as this species of trout was considered the chief offender in the destruction of salmon spawn and the young fish. However, recent conclusions seem to indicate that this upset another important part of nature's balancing, and the stickleback—a small fish that feeds upon the same food as salmon fry—increased more rapidly as the Dolly Vardens were thinned down. Therefore, the bounty was withdrawn and Dolly Varden trout now are protected as a game fish throughout most of Alaska.

The length of time young salmon spend in the fresh-water creeks varies greatly with the species, but the young fish eventually find their way to salt water where they remain for one or more years, feeding and growing rapidly, the length of time depending upon the species.

Where the salmon spends its maturing years while in salt water is an unsolved mystery. But once it has reached maturity it returns unerringly to the stream where it was hatched, to spawn and die. It is an established fact that Pacific salmon spawn only once, and that all of them die in the spawning stream except a few which spawn near salt water and drift down stream to die in the near-by salt-water bay or inlet.

An adult salmon produces from two to five thousand eggs, the number depending upon the species and size of the fish. All except the king and silver salmon are said to subsist upon minute organisms in the water throughout their entire life. The king and silver feed upon insects and small fishes and respond readily to plugs, spoons, and bait in the bays and even in fresh-water streams as they approach the spawning beds.

In well-protected areas salmon ascend the streams in such great numbers that they sometimes actually crowd each other in their struggles to overcome waterfalls and other hazards. Nearly every species of carnivorous animal and many birds of prey gather along the streams in spawning season to feast upon the struggling fish and upon the dead fish that line the banks of Alaska's creeks and rivers.

The flesh of the salmon is very rich in proteins, fats, and vitamins and is highly suitable for canning. Although large quantities are sold fresh and frozen, the bulk of the annual catch is canned.

These excellent food fish vary a great deal in size. Fully grown kings have been known to weigh as much as 125 pounds. The average is about 23 pounds, but fish from 40 to 60 pounds are quite common. The time spent in salt water likewise varies from one to four years. King salmon placed in fresh-water lakes where they cannot reach the ocean grow to maturity and reach a large size. They are found in Alaskan waters throughout the year, with the heaviest runs from spring to fall.

The red salmon spends two to four years in salt water, and the average weight is about six pounds. They sometimes become landlocked and are called by the natives "silver trout," "Kokanee," and "little red fish." The time of the run varies in different localities.

The silver spends one to two years in salt water after spending one or two years in fresh water. The average weight is about nine and one-half pounds. Their runs occur chiefly in the late summer and fall, from July to October.

The pink salmon, greatest in number in Alaska, matures at the age of two years, after one year in fresh water and one in salt water. They average about three to four pounds in weight. Their runs vary in different districts but usually occur from June to September.

The chum matures in from two to five years, and eighteen months to four years of its life are spent in salt water. The average weight of a mature fish is about nine pounds, but extra large fish weighing up to forty-five pounds are not unusual. Their runs occur from late spring to late fall.

There is romance aplenty in nature's unusual pattern for the lives of salmon: the struggles and hardships they undergo to overcome every obstacle in order to attain the same spawning grounds where they themselves were hatched; the vicious and continuous fights between male salmon to establish and maintain exclusive favor with their chosen mate; and their rendezvous with certain death once they have ended their spawning and have assured perpetuation of their species.

And there is still more romance, and plenty of work too, in the vast industry flung along the Pacific Coast from Oregon to the far reaches of Alaska. In the salmon industry men gamble their money, their futures, and even their lives, to catch and prepare this appetizing and nourishing food fish.

When springtime comes to the Pacific Coast the salmon fleet begins to stir. Some two thousand boats are checked over, seams recalked, new paint is applied, engines and gear get a thorough overhauling, and the fleet is readied for the silver harvest soon to be reaped. From as far away as Seattle many steamers and smaller boats, loaded with cans, materials for cases, machinery, fishing gear, and other necessities of the canning season, including men—Alaska cannot supply all the manpower needed—head for Alaska waters. From every town and village throughout the entire length of the far-flung Alaska coast line boats put out for favored spots.

Salmon are taken by trollers and purse seiners on the high seas; by fish traps, seines, and gill nets in the coastal waters, and by drift and anchored gill nets in the larger rivers.

Traps made of piling with webbing that forms net-inclosed compartments take many fish. This webbing is so arranged that the fish enter but are unable to find their way out. By use of a "brailer"—a kind of apron in most cases and basket in others—hundreds of fish are lifted from the trap and dumped into the hold of the waiting boat and rapidly transported to the cannery.

The purse seine is used to encircle a school of salmon, and pull ropes tighten the seine until a "purse" is formed, and the salmon thus are drawn into a smaller and smaller space and eventually dumped into the boat.

Beach seines are similarly used, except that they encircle a school of fish from the shore, and the seine and fish are beached.

Gill nets are set across the path of swimming salmon in silt-laden water, and the fish are enmeshed. The mesh is large enough to permit undersized fish to escape.

Trolling boats are everywhere. They are a familiar sight during the salmon season, even along isolated stretches of the inner passage, with their heavy wooden poles protruding from each side and from the rear. A long line extends from each pole, and a spoon or other lure or bait is trolled to lure the fish. Salmon taken in this manner—kings and silvers—are usually mild-cured, used fresh, or quick-frozen, as they are taken in prime condition, dressed, and sold by the pound rather than by the fish as trap- or net-taken fish are usually sold. While trap and seine fishing are confined to relatively short periods, trolling is permitted throughout most of the year.

Fish wheels—wheels with a scooplike attachment—are used along some of the inland rivers for taking fish for personal use and for dog food. The natives often use this method to catch salmon. They dry the fish on racks for winter use.

Hundreds of boats and scows dock every day along the cannery wharves. Various methods of unloading the fish are employed, but the most effective manner of accomplishing this job is to wash them from the decks into the escalator—commonly called elevator—by using a heavy stream of water. Next comes the sorting process, where they are sorted as to species and placed in their respective bins. A heavily painted smooth surface permits thorough cleaning of these bins, and they are kept scrupulously clean.

From the bins the fish are conveyed by chute and belt or chain conveyer to the "Iron Chinks" for cleaning. This unique machine acquired its name from the custom of early canneries of hiring Chinese to clean the fish. It works with humanlike precision and many times faster. After the head has been removed by a mechanical cutter, a workman places the fish in position and the machine does the rest, removing the tail, fins, and scales, slitting open and scrubbing the body cavity, while the offal is swept away by brushes. The Iron Chink prepares from sixty to eighty-five fish a minute.

Next comes the cutting and filling, and here again the work is precisely done by machinery. Cans, which usually are shipped flattened out in the same cases that transport the filled cans throughout the world, are quickly rounded into shape and the bottoms fastened on. With almost uncanny accuracy a machine cuts the fish in pieces to fit into the can, and the cans are filled to weigh exactly the amount required. Each can as it is filled travels over a conveyer where it is weighed automatically, and any underweight cans are shunted aside and go to the patching table where additional pieces of fish are placed in the can, and the can is then hand-weighed. Over a hundred cans a minute are thus packed.

Throughout the entire operations described above the fish are untouched by human hands. When it is necessary to handle them as they are placed in the machines, and where improperly filled cans are correctly filled and reweighed, workmen wear gloves.

The packed cans are conveyed automatically to a vacuum-sealing machine where they are sealed under pressure, and from there they go to the huge pressure cookers called retorts.

There the salmon are cooked for an hour and twenty minutes under some 240 degrees of heat. Then the cans are labeled and packed, and the long trip begins to grocery shelves all over the world.

Besides salmon, herring and halibut are the principal food fish taken in Alaska waters. Fleets of halibut boats, fully manned and with ice facilities for preserving the catch, leave Seattle and Alaska ports each year for the halibut grounds off the Alaska coast. Halibut is sold fresh or quick-frozen and shipped to markets throughout the world, and a better eating fish is hard to find than a fresh "chicken halibut"—a fish of eight or ten pounds in weight. Mediums—ten to sixty pounds —are said to command nearly twice the price of other size fish, as they make the size slices preferred by restaurants.

Halibut are found in abundance in the straits, bays, and inlets along Alaska's coast and in the Gulf of Alaska. Fish weighing over a hundred pounds are sometimes caught with rod and reel from the docks at Cordova and other coast towns.

A rapidly expanding market for fresh fish, owing to the quick marketing facilities made possible by air transportation, is opening up vast new fields in the Alaska fishing industry.

Before the war more than half of the crab meat consumed in the United States was imported, and approximately 95 per cent of the canned crab likewise was imported, most of it from Japan. Successful canning operations of shrimp, clams, and crabs are now carried on in Petersburg and Cordova, and Wrangell is soon to have a crab line for vacuum-packing crab meat. Many species of shellfish, including the butter clams, the Dungeness crab, king or spider crab, and a small variety of the much-prized abalone, could be produced in much larger quantities.

A new fishing industry was begun recently in Ketchikan for processing of species not previously used to any great extent, including sole, gray cod, rock cod, red snapper, ling cod, kelp cod, and other fish, which will be marketed in fillet and steak form in one- and five-pound packages.

An enormous volume of offal from Alaska canneries is at present being dumped into the ocean. This waste material is rich in vitamins for production of fish meal, oils, fertilizer, and other by-products and can be obtained in sufficient quantities in localities where a number of canneries are located to make such operations profitable.

A recent and highly valuable addition to Alaska's commercial fisheries is the taking of sharks and dogfish. The livers and meat of sharks and the livers of dogfish bring good prices. The livers are used in the manufacture of vitamin A and liver extracts. Shark meat is coming into its own as a food; it is of good texture and flavor and highly nutritious.

Experiments are now under way toward utilization of sharkskin for leather substitutes. The Fishery Products Laboratory at Ketchikan has some excellent fishskin samples that resemble heavy leather. They are of beautiful texture and soft and pliable. Because of the abundance of both sharks and dogfish and the year-round possibilities of this new industry in southern and southeastern Alaska, taking of these fish is a profitable adjunct to other commercial fishing and is fast becoming an industry in its own right.

Disabled veterans might investigate the possibilities of processing and canning, on a small scale, fancy-packed smoked king and silver salmon and preserving and canning additional quantities of salmon eggs for bait. Most of the eggs are discarded at present, although some already are being preserved. Along this line are possibilities for handmade lures, tackle, boats, and other fishing equipment to supply the ever increasing demand of newcomers to the Territory.

While the fishing industry is not to be considered an open field for newcomers, experienced commercial fishermen might profit by investigating the possibilities. Before the war it was possible to buy a one-man trolling boat with all necessary equipment for two to four thousand dollars. The value of a normal year's trolling catch usually runs, after expenses are paid, from two to four thousand dollars.

From the time the first cannery was established in Klawock about 1878 to the peak year of 1936 when 8,454,000 cases were produced, and even to 1946 with a past ten-year average of 5,475,000 cases, many problems have confronted the commercial fishing industry, especially in the matter of regulation. It soon became evident, when commercial fishing began to expand, that total depletion of the supply in a certain area would result from barricading spawning streams. This resulted in a prohibition against such practices in 1889, followed by elimination of commercial fishing in streams. This was followed in short order by regulations governing weekly closed periods, restricted areas, submission of reports by operators, setting up of proper enforcement machinery, taxation, prohibiting alien fishing; regulation of fishing gear, seasons, escapement; authorizing seizure of gear for violations, etc. Also regulation of halibut fishing, herring fishing, and the taking of clams, crabs, and other fish and shellfish.

A sixty-three-page booklet, *Laws and Regulations for Protection of the Commercial Fisheries of Alaska*, may be obtained from the U.S. Fish and Wildlife Service, U.S. Department of the Interior, Juneau, Alaska. It is impractical to condense this regulation here as it has too many ramifications and is subject to periodic changes.

Since 1940 all enforcement and supervisory machinery has been consolidated under the Fish and Wildlife Service through consolidation of the former Bureau of Fisheries and the Bureau of Biological Survey, with local offices in the principal towns throughout Alaska. The three operative subdivisions of the service concerned with Alaska fisheries under the national headquarters office are as follows:

Division of Alaska Fisheries—Fish and Fur Seal

Division of Fishery, Biology

Division of Commercial Fisheries

Their duties are many and varied, including regulating, enforcement, statistics, stream surveys, operation of counting weirs, basis for setting seasons and importance of adjustment of these seasons to meet changing dates of runs, particularly with respect to pinks and chums; study of conditions affecting reproduction and survival in fresh water, conditions affecting survival in salt water, amount of seeding required to produce best results for given streams, routes and periods of migration, etc. This same Fish and Wildlife Service is responsible for supervision and enforcement of laws covering all other salt-water commercial fishing, also sport fishing, hunting, and trapping.

It is claimed by those in authority that expansion of the activities of this department, which has been static for some time due to lack of funds, would probably increase production of this important food industry as much as 25 per cent. Such expansion is impossible without additional finances, as neither the funds nor personnel are sufficient at present to carry on any program except a skeleton patrol during the fishing season and limited scientific investigations. Since this industry is now contributing over a million dollars a year in territorial and federal taxes, to say nothing of corporation, business, and personal taxes, and the federal government's expenditure has averaged less than one third that amount, there seems no good reason why a very substantial increase in financing should not be allowed.

Canada's appropriation for approximately one third as much coast line is said to be three times as much as our own.

It should be of special interest to every person and civic organization in the Territory, as well as people in the States who likewise have an interest in Alaska's fishing industry, to insist upon broadened and improved methods of conservation of Alaska's fishing resources.

Increased demands for fish and fish products have encouraged improved methods of capture and processing of fish. And this same increased demand has encouraged violations of regulations. In recent years the use of airplane and radio in connection with creek robbing of salmon streams has entered the picture. A small radio-equipped plane keeps watch as illegal fishing proceeds, and upon the approach of an agent or a patrol boat, the alarm is radioed to violators, which gives them ample time to escape before they can be apprehended. Plenty of patrol planes will stop this.

Making a higher penalty mandatory upon conviction would materially assist enforcement officials in their efforts to enforce properly commercial fishing laws. It is discouraging to enforcement officials and tends to increase violations that only light fines are assessed against convicted violators. In a great many instances convicted violators receive sentences so light that they are out of all proportion when compared with the time and effort expended by enforcement officials in accumulating the information with which to convict them.

On account of the increase in numbers of radio-equipped fishing boats a school of salmon has a poor chance to get through to the spawning beds. These boats radio to other boats the spot where fish are plentiful, which enables them to congregate and clean up the school of salmon before any number of them can escape to the safety of the spawning creek.

One small plane in southeastern Alaska is used as a combined Fisheries and Game patrol ship, and the job is much more than one plane can handle.

Says Mr. Emery F. Tobin in an editorial in the *Alaska Sportsman*:

> There are scores of salmon streams in the Ketchikan district, but during the past few years Congress has provided funds for only five watchmen in this district. The result has been that illegal fishing has resulted in the taking of nearly every salmon during the open season except at the five streams where watchmen were maintained. There is great need for increased appropriations by Congress in order that men and equipment to conserve the salmon fisheries in southeastern Alaska may be increased. There certainly is need for more enforcement personnel and equipment, and perhaps equally important, greater observance of the laws and regulations by those directly involved in this most important of all Alaska industries.

The result of proper patrolling of one of those southeastern Alaska streams is reported by Milton Orton, who has lived for thirty years on the Naha River twenty-five miles from Ketchikan, as quoted in the same editorial as follows:

> I have seen the sockeye run drop from well over 100,000 fish on this stream down to 7,000 to 8,000 in

the early 1920's, and have seen it gradually build up a run of 100,000 to 125,000 fish in 1944, and 175,000 in 1945.

The first sockeye salmon are in the river around June 20th and the biggest part of the run is in the river and lakes by July 15th when commercial fishing has opened here during the past several years. During open season for salmon there is a closed period for all commercial salmon from 6:00 Saturday evening each week until 6:00 of the following Monday morning.

Each Monday and Tuesday there are several thousand salmon at the head of Naha Bay. These fish all get into the river. This river has had a watchman for about twenty years, and the salmon run has been building up about that time because of this protection.

Dr. Ira N. Gabrielson, former national director of Fish and Wildlife Service, declared recently in Juneau, according to the *Alaska Weekly*, that the decreasing salmon catches in southeastern Alaska would require the co-operation of all concerned for solution. He pointed out that for three successive years southeastern Alaska runs have been very poor and that there are no indications that would give reason for expecting improvements.

Lack of enforcement and inability of agents to check on salmon runs in each locality has created considerable controversy relative to seasons. A great many fishermen claim that the salmon season should be flexible enough to permit taking fish when the fish are there for the taking; that the largest run of salmon often occurs after the arbitrary closing date; that the salmon have a way of observing water temperature and other natural phenomena rather than man-made fish-taking dates and are often not at all co-operative in the matter. There can be little doubt that some justification exists for their complaint, especially in view of the established fact that too much escapement and overseeding does not bring about the optimum production of salmon.

Likewise, the halibut fishermen claim that the ever shortening halibut season is depriving them of the taking of certain nonmigratory stocks of halibut of smaller but marketable sizes, and possibly part of the stocks of larger-size halibut in some localities.

Commercial fishing is vital to the very life of Alaska's present economy. And commercial fish, especially salmon—unlike inanimate things such as minerals or metals, which are exploited until the supply is exhausted and do not reproduce—if properly supervised to permit escapement of sufficient seeding stock, will continue to reproduce bountifully, and an increasing catch may be enjoyed in the years to come.

This industry needs no promoting. It already enjoys first place in Alaska industry. Why then must appropriations for the financing of supervision and enforcement be *decreased* from $457,868.84 in 1931 to $397,906.00 in 1946, during a period when operating costs of all other government departments, almost without exception, have *increased*?

How much this decrease in finances, and corresponding lack of ability to enforce regulations, has contributed to the decrease in the Bristol Bay red-salmon catch which has occurred in every cycle year except one since 1934, nobody knows. Or how much the lack of funds and enforcement has contributed to the Alaska Peninsula's low three-year catch and southeastern Alaska's recent poor years is also a matter of conjecture.

And unless a sound program of management is adopted and

funds made available to place it in operation, it is entirely possible that Alaska's salmon resource will decline even more from its present state of productivity. If it becomes depleted or even partially depleted, Alaska's future is indeed dark. This should be taken into account when consideration is given the spending of one, two, or even three million dollars a year. It is not too much to pay to preserve Alaska's tremendous fisheries resources.

CHAPTER TEN

Possibilities, People, and Development

EVERY Alaska-bound boat that nowadays pulls away from an American or near-by Canadian port is loaded to the gunwale with merchandise and equipment, and every available passenger space is occupied. Huge passenger planes and transports roar away with capacity loads. The miniature stampede toward the Territory that began even before the cessation of hostilities in World War II now has begun to assume the proportions of a possible avalanche.

This sudden desire of hundreds of thousands of people in the States to go to Alaska is remarkable in that it was not encouraged by the government, which owns nearly all the land in the Territory; neither was it instigated by the people of Alaska, who do not want a boom. The impetus came almost entirely from *without*.

Great numbers of Americans—Army and Navy personnel and construction workers—have in recent years seen with their own eyes the opportunities offered by this young and vigorous territory of ours. They have talked with restaurant owners, farmers, fishermen, and other small businessmen that came to Alaska with only a few hundred dollars and are well on their way to financial success despite the many problems, handicaps, and hardships of a new frontier country. They have seen Alaska's tremendous commercial and recreational resources, enough to support an empire of several million people. They have absorbed a portion of that indescribable urge—that spell of the great north country—that seems to pull one back to Alaska once he has spent some time there. There is a saying in Alaska that a newcomer usually is dissatisfied during his first year, will always have a yearning to return to Alaska if he leaves during his second year, and will not leave Alaska if he stays into the third year.

It is difficult for anyone that is not familiar with the Territory to understand why Alaska with such vast resources has not followed the usual pattern of rapid orderly development, why, after approximately eighty years of United States ownership, there are today fewer than a hundred thousand people in Alaska; and why it has taken a world war and the invasion of our far-flung territory to start the wheels of migration rolling. A brief retrospective look at Alaska's development since we purchased the Territory in 1867 will enlighten us somewhat.

Little incentive existed for settlement of Alaska during the twenty odd years following its purchase. Millions of acres of fertile land in the States were then available for homesteading or for purchase at low prices. The distance to Alaska in that day of horse-drawn locomotion and the fact that there was no overland route to the Territory further discouraged settlement.

Then came the gold rush, a truly spectacular migration! Thousands from the States, even from foreign countries, converged upon Alaska. Few, if any, of the gold-rush pioneers had any intention of remaining in Alaska. They had visions of scooping up all the gold they could pack out, returning to the States, and living happily ever after. But regardless of whatever may have been the intentions of the gold seekers about remaining permanently in Alaska, a goodly number of them settled there, and many families living in the Territory today are the offspring of the original gold seekers, whose ranks have thinned with time although there are a surprising number still to be found there.

During the gold-rush decade from 1890 to 1900, the population of Alaska nearly doubled, from 32,052 to 63,592. The fact that during the next thirty-year period the Territory just about held this tremendous boom increase is without parallel in the annals of population statistics. Continued mineral production, furs, and the advent and development of commercial fishing each contributed its share toward maintaining Alaska's boom population figure.

From 1930 to 1940 Alaska enjoyed a steady healthy growth —an increase of some 20 per cent to slightly over 70,000. During that period agriculture, which theretofore had been largely confined to produce gardens and an occasional farm, expanded under the impetus of the government-sponsored Matanuska project to a definite place in Alaska industry. Commercial fishing, mining, lumbering, and the fur industry advanced apace with agriculture.

Next came the chaotic war period with its tremendous spurt in Alaska's transient and permanent population, followed by the postwar rush of newcomers to the Territory, limited only by inferior and totally inadequate transportation services from the States to Alaska and by Alaska's ability to absorb the influx of new settlers.

There is no doubt that Alaska's development, especially in recent years, has been retarded and still is being retarded by too much federal administrative power and too little territorial self-government. Under the present system Alaska elects a territorial legislature, but it has extremely limited powers. No law may be passed "... interfering with the primary disposal of the soil." In fact, no law may be passed affecting anything, except it be approved by a federally appointed governor, and if it successfully negotiates that hurdle, it must then be approved by Congress. Alaska also elects a delegate to Congress that may enter a bill and participate in debate, but *he has no vote*. Anyone at all conversant with legislative procedure must appreciate his handicap. Alaska's three divisions of government—executive, legislative, and judicial—are overshadowed with a fourth division—administrative, "... which has to do with the 99 per cent of land, water and natural resources remaining in the hands of the Federal Government."

With no county government and with territorial powers limited, the administrative branch—federal—is all-powerful.

The question of aboriginal rights—the land, mineral, and hunting and fishing rights of the Indians and Eskimos—said to have been resurrected by the Department of the Interior during the Ickes regime, still remains unsettled. And while little irreparable damage has been done, until the question is settled it will continue to cloud the title to considerable valuable land and fishing rights in Alaska, and will tend to retard Alaska development.

The government's strangle hold on Alaska's land seems to have let up a bit under the administration of Secretary of the Interior Krug, and the people of Alaska are jubilant because of his quick understanding of Alaska's problems and his immediate steps to solve them. One of his first acts, after a careful survey of the Alaska situation, was to announce the return and opening for entry of 18,000,000 acres of public land in the Alaska Peninsula and the Katalla-Yakataga regions, land which had been set aside by the government in 1943. He also announced that the five-mile strip reserved along either side of the Alaska Highway was soon to be reduced to three hundred feet.

There are indications that Secretary Krug is keenly aware that some relaxation is in order of regulations which now prevent outright sale of public lands. Many Alaskans believe that the solution of Alaska's development problem lies in the outright sale, instead of lease, to pulp manufacturers, ranchers, sawmill owners, prospective lodge builders, and others of tracts of land sufficient for the needs of such enterprises. Attractive offers to lease acreage for such industries have failed, while at the same time every block of patented land suitable for such industries has been eagerly snapped up. Individual ownership—not government ownership—is the American way, so that the investment and good will may be handed down from father to son, and not have to revert after a time to government ownership again.

Another serious drawback to Alaska development, for which no solution is in sight, is the upset economy of the Territory. Unusually high transportation rates by water, and even higher rates on the government-owned Alaska Railroad, make for high labor costs; and high labor costs make competitive manufacturing for outside consumption difficult. The minimum for unskilled Alaska labor today is about a dollar an hour, which is consistent with a haircut at a dollar, shave seventy-five cents, and ham and eggs eighty-five cents to a dollar. high rates

Pulp manufacturers that must invest ten to fifteen million dollars in a plant are aware of Canada's pulp plants going full blast a short distance down the coast, with lower freight costs and a wage scale of eighty-two cents per hour. They likewise are aware that this eighty-two cents in Canada will buy as much or more than the Alaska dollar when expended in Alaska. In Canada the same haircut is fifty cents, shave twenty-five cents, and ham and eggs forty-five cents.

Apparently Alaska was labor-organized at least twenty-five years too soon for a developing, but largely undeveloped, community. On account of Alaska fisheries, which necessitated the importation of much outside union labor, unions gained an early foothold, which they have expanded even to the Eskimos and Indians that work in the fisheries. Thus an unusually high wage scale is maintained in Alaska, which is all right so long as Alaska has no desire to compete with outside production except on certain commodities, such as salmon, that are short elsewhere. If Alaska's minimum wage scale remains at a dollar, and the Alaska barber takes the dollar for the Alaska haircut, and the cleaner takes two dollars of the barber's money for cleaning his suit, nobody gets hurt (or helped) and money circulates freely within the Territory. But with the afore-mentioned Canadian economy offering near-by competition, and with southern pine with its fast rotation period being turned into pulp in the southern states with a sixty-five-cent wage scale, and the haircut thirty-five cents in that area, so far as pulp is concerned Alaska cannot compete.

To add still further to Alaska's economic woes, war and government mismanagement combined to create such a state of "snafu" in Alaska steamship transportation that the steamship companies have been forced to refuse acceptance of the return of their lines. Under this war government control, the unions were granted just about everything they asked, and ordinary discipline of crew members was not enforced by either the government or the unions. The result was a tremendous loss during such control, said to total over five million dollars in one year on one steamship line, and the quality of

service worsened in about the same proportion that costs increased. In an attempt to induce the steamship owners to
resume control, the government is said to have offered them
an increase, in the already excessively high Alaska shipping
rates, of 80 per cent or more; but even that inducement,
which would be absolutely ruinous to Alaska, was not enough
with the state of almost total disintegration of system, service,
and authority. The steamship companies pointed out that since
1939 ship crews and officers have had wage increases of 90
per cent while rates have increased only 16 per cent.

Says the *Alaska Weekly* in an editorial referring to proposed water-borne freight rates:

> If such an increase, with corresponding increases in
> passenger rates should be made effective, we can forget
> Alaska development and write the Territory off as a
> loss, for it shortly will be depopulated.... The various
> unions involved have contrived to tremendously in-
> crease costs while decreasing revenue. Inefficiency,
> drunkenness and pilfering of cargo have been the rule
> rather than the exception. Even these have been petty
> annoyances as compared to the slow-down methods
> employed which have increased the round-trip time
> from Seattle to Seward from 12 to anywhere from 14
> to 19 days, thus increasing the cost per trip at least 25
> per cent.
>
> The heavy losses resulting from this type of opera-
> tion have been absorbed by the War Shipping Admin-
> istration, which, of course, means the taxpayer. But the
> time approaches when the War Shipping Administra-
> tion will step out of the picture and lay the sorry mess
> in the lap of private interests. These private interests

do not have a key to the United States' Treasury . . . and they would need it to keep the ships running at the present rates.

The one bright spot in Alaska's dark transportation picture is that several million dollars' worth of new equipment has been secured for the Alaska Railroad. This, together with a revamping of its program, is expected to reduce transportation costs over this vital line.

The reindeer industry, which furnishes (or once did furnish) the principal meat supply from Nome northward and was an economic factor in the development of the north country comparable to beef cattle in Chicago, Kansas City, or Fort Worth, has at last been returned to the Eskimo. According to an editorial in the *Alaska Sportsman—*

> The reindeer industry was turned over to the Department of the Interior (1940) and that department has since had full control. What is the result? Whereas the herds once totaled 600,000 deer (some say more than a million), their numbers have been decimated until now the total is only 65,000. (Feeding grounds for 4,000,000 head are said to exist.) Herding has been practically abandoned. Wolves have had full sway and have torn the herds to shreds. An industry which meant so much to the Eskimos and which cost a million dollars to build up is all but gone.

It is believed that pride of ownership, now that the herds are again in the hands of Eskimo owners, will encourage the Eskimo to protect them, even as he protected them before government control, and that now the depleted herds will stage a comeback. Otherwise this disastrous experiment in government control will necessitate the expenditure of millions for relief among the Eskimos.

Few people outside of the Territory are able to conceive of Alaska's inaccessibility, distances, climate, and other features utterly incomparable with anything in the States. State governments function in the forty-eight states to eliminate exactly the difficulties Alaska is experiencing, especially as regards natural resources and development within the Territory. It would seem therefore that the only solution in sight is statehood for the Territory.

If statehood comes to Alaska, with it will come certain definite obligations. Alaska will have to provide facilities that the people require for economic and social development and the financial resources to procure and maintain them. Some of these requirements are provided by the Territory now.

Incidentally, statehood would not necessarily mean that Alaska would immediately fall heir to *all* government-owned land in Alaska. Certain reservations which have been set aside would be reserved to the federal government for disposal under congressional direction, in the same manner that such reservations have been handled in some other new states admitted to the Union.

Principal objections to statehood seem to focus around the tax issue. Some argue that with Alaska's present population—estimated at 85,000—over a third of which is native, Alaska could not finance itself as a state. Others point to Alaska's lack of markets for its agricultural products, also Alaska's seasonal job opportunities. These same handicaps were met and overcome by other states in their infancy, but none was of such immense size as Alaska, and none was so rugged and inaccessible; and, first and foremost, none suffered the present tremendous handicap of inflation and union control of wages.

How such control effectively retards development in Alaska was well illustrated in the recent abortive attempt to inaugurate a badly needed coastal steamship line to further Alaska's tourist trade and provide additional market facilities. This line died a-borning when the unions were said to have demanded so much that the steamship line could not possibly make a profit, and the project was abandoned.

All objections to statehood have some basis in fact, yet none of them, collectively or singly, constitute an insurmountable obstacle to statehood. A substantial proportion of the people of Alaska argue that Alaska is all right just as it is, does not need rapid development; and they do not relish state property taxes. They believe that rapid development and the influx of many new settlers will quickly kill out or chase into inaccessible regions the big game of Alaska, thus depriving the present inhabitants of the pleasure of the near-by fall hunt and the winter meat supply such game now affords. Another substantial proportion of the people of Alaska say that it is the spirit of America to go forward with development and that Alaska cannot get a fair proportion of federal highway appropriations and other funds necessary for Alaska's development without voting representation in the nation's capital. They also assert that statehood is not only desirable but indispensable to the welfare, development, and progress of Alaska and the defense of the Territory and the nation.

Governor Gruening said in a talk at Fairbanks recently, "We have only partial citizenship so long as we remain a Territory." Secretary Krug also endorses statehood. However, two of a group of touring congressmen discouraged statehood upon their return to Washington from Alaska not long ago with the statement that Alaska is "not yet ready." Exactly what they were referring to is not known, in view of the

fact that Missouri, Illinois, Oregon, Nevada, and Wyoming
had less population than Alaska now has when they were
admitted to statehood, and several other states had fewer
than a hundred thousand population when admitted. And it
is an incontrovertible fact that the people in Alaska are today far better educated, informed, and more capable of self-
government than were the people of most other territories
when they became states. A recent editorial in the *Alaska
Sportsman* called attention to the fact that Alaska has nearly
twice the national average of college-educated inhabitants,
and the percentage of high-school graduates is also relatively
high.

There are other things that Alaska should do toward put-
ting its own house in order if it is to assume the responsibili-
ties that go with statehood. The liquor situation throughout
the Territory is deplorable. With nearly five hundred
liquor outlets, Alaska supports one liquor store for approximately each 170 inhabitants—men, women, and children. The
situation became so serious that a recent federal grand jury
recommended drastic changes in liquor laws and enforcement.

Liquor sellers in Alaska will do well to heed the present
signs that point toward prohibition. They should be the first
to inaugurate necessary reforms to keep drunkenness and its
attendant evils within due bounds. And they are not now
within due bounds.

The majority of the good people of Alaska, as elsewhere,
do not use liquor to excess, but the unbridled overindulgence
of a minority is adversely affecting the interests of everyone, has materially added to the accident and crime per-
centages, has increased absenteeism out of all proportion, and
should be curbed, and soon.

Alaska cannot avoid a uniform tax program if statehood is accepted. An educator in Alaska said recently that what the Territory needs most is a uniform tax program and competition. A mechanic expressed almost the identical thought when he asserted that what Alaska needs most is more roads and a good twenty-five-cent bowl of chili. Yet, a great many Alaskans still want a Santa Claus. They want the freedom and development to which Alaska is entitled, but they do not want to dig down and pay for them.

Some Alaskans do not seem to realize that the old, complacent manner of living must give way to the ingenuity of man and to the unfilled desires for new frontiers to settle of thousands of people that will not be denied. Complacency invites all kinds of settlement schemes such as that recently advanced by former secretary of the Interior Ickes in his magazine article, "Let's Open Up Alaska!" wherein he advocated settlement of Alaska by foreigners. His implication that Americans are too "soft" to withstand the rigors and hardships of frontier Alaska was refuted almost before the ink dried by the influx of hundreds of new settlers. Alaska will welcome its proportion of suitable immigrants in exactly the same ratio that Mr. Ickes' home state and the other divisions of the United States will absorb them; and that is all.

Alaskans represent some of the best pioneer-blooded Americans to be found anywhere, and they wholeheartedly resent having Alaska considered an out-of-the-way, unimportant dumping ground—a sort of half-formed subdivision of the United States.

There are business opportunities for many Americans in Alaska right now, in spite of handicaps. And it is safe to assert that Americans will take advantage of every opportunity offered.

Alaska needs certain types of skilled American laborers—carpenters, painters, plumbers, electricians, clerical help (preferably male), stenographers, salespeople (grocery, hardware, and clothing), sawmill workers, bakers, automobile mechanics and body men, skilled laundry workers, printers, mine workers. It should be borne in mind that only a limited number of each of these skills is needed in each town, and it would be wise to inquire of the local territorial employment office in the different towns throughout the Territory before going to Alaska.

Teachers are needed in industrial arts, mathematics, science, physical education, also qualified rural teachers. Rural teachers are employed by the Superintendent of the Department of Education, Territory of Alaska, Juneau. The local board employs city teachers, with authority usually delegated to the superintendent of the board.

Alaska also has need of doctors, dentists, jewelers—especially jewelry manufacturers—optometrists, oculists, and other professional people. Inquiry may be made to the chambers of commerce.

Alaska has room for more small-town preachers and more churches. There are some forty Russian-Greek Orthodox churches in the villages of Alaska, and some of each of the usual denominations prevalent in the States are to be found in most towns, but the posted directories in the towns reveal an unexpected absence of one or more churches common to towns of like size in the States.

Alaska's prospects for straightening out some of her tangled problems are beginning to brighten. Secretary Krug's recent announcement of a seven-point plan for Alaska, some of which already is materializing, includes: (1) a campaign to induce business interests to invest capital in the Territory;

Stretched beaver pelts. Very large ones are called "blankets."
(*Copyright The Alaska Sportsman*)

A trapper's cabin and some pelts. (*Copyright The Alaska Sportsman*)

An Alaska trapper and his winter's catch. (*Copyright The Alaska Sportsman*)

Dozens of canneries, such as this one at Kasaan, dot the shores of Alaska's coast line. (*Copyright Forest Service*)

Prospecting for gold. Alaska needs experienced prospectors to develop practically unlimited mineral resources. (*Copyright Forest Service*)

Alaska Juneau Mine. Gold mining has been one of Alaska's principal industries for many years. (*Copyright Forest Service*)

Commercial fishing provides seasonal employment for some 25,000 people in Alaska. Nets, seines, traps, and trolling take large quantities of fish. (*Copyright The Alaska Sportsman*)

Hotels in Alaska compare favorably with those in much larger cities in the States. Bubble Room, Hotel Baranof, Juneau. (*Photo by Paul, Jr.*)

(2) ways and means to make Alaska a full partner of the United States with a greater measure of self-government; (3) studies by business and labor concerning Alaska's industrial development; (4) development of the tourist industry by making public land available along the Alaska Highway and improved tourist facilities throughout the Territory, also improved roads; (5) greater agricultural development through soil surveys and crop recommendations, better marketing conditions, and farm credit possibilities; (6) an increased public works program; (7) improvement of government administrative services in Alaska.

Recent appropriations for additional roads into heretofore isolated regions, including the Fortymile and Kenai-Homer areas, will make accessible rich mining and agricultural districts. However, much more federal money for road building and upkeep is needed if Alaska is to prosper. Badly needed when construction funds will permit is a road extending from the Richardson Highway near Paxson Lodge to the McKinley National Park area, which will open up an area that is tremendously important for its minerals and metals as well as for recreation. That portion of the Haines Highway within the Territory needs considerable improvement if it is to serve as the terminus of a ferry service from the States and British Columbia ports to inland Alaska. There is tremendous need of a Fairbanks-Nome road, Nome-Teller road, Ophir-Ruby road, and Chena–Hot Springs road, which would open up rich mining, potential agricultural, and recreational areas.

With territorial road construction limited owing to the necessity of financing the many social benefits that were absent during the movement of civilization westward to the Pacific, such as education, pensions, public health, and welfare projects, Alaska must look to the federal government for road funds. This certainly is not unreasonable when it is recognized that approximately 98 per cent of the whole of Alaska is owned by the federal government, and federal money used on roads is developing federally owned land.

Alaska does not share in the funds of the Federal Highway Act, while the territories of Hawaii and Puerto Rico are given this benefit. Today, the greatest hindrance to agricultural development in Alaska is inaccessibility to markets.

A proper building and expansion program is badly needed to ensure the continuation of Alaska's vital commercial fishing industry, and according to Alaskan ichthyologists, it should include the following: ten biological stations and equipment; seven research vessels, 36 x 90 feet; nine aircraft; one tender, for delivery of supplies and equipment, 130 x 150 feet long; thirty-seven patrol boats, 36 x 45 feet; reconditioning of the present fleet; construction and equipping of necessary marine stations, warehouses, docks, aircraft hangers, and other facilities required for storage and maintenance of vessels, aircraft, and equipment; construction and operation of weirs for checking escapement; construction and operation of fishways, or ladders, where required; clearance of barriers in spawning streams; personnel to operate and maintain equipment properly and to supervise properly fishing operations and enforce laws.

It is estimated that the cost of this program would total about $2,700,000. This amount could be spread over a five-year period. An annual maintenance cost of approximately $850,000 would be required to continue the program upon completion of the installations.

This does not seem to be too much to expend for perpetuation of an industry that produces $55,000,000 a year and employs 25,000 people. And with proper facilities and management, this production and employment can be increased some 25 per cent.

Vital to Alaska air transportation is her radio-telephone communication system, now operating between all cities in the Territory, between all principal airfields, and to the States.

Also of tremendous importance are the hundreds of individual operators, affectionately referred to as "ham" operators, scattered throughout Alaska, especially in the isolated regions. Restrictions were removed some time ago, and now the once familiar newsy items that originate everywhere in the Territory where no other communication exists are coming in—the urgent call for medical assistance on account of the unexpected early arrival of a new baby, the need for antitoxin when a diphtheria epidemic threatens, the hurried call for a piece for broken machinery, the idle chatter of two lonesome hams. Important weather information, broadcast by schoolteachers, employees of the Bureau of Indian Affairs, trading post operators, and by individuals who have their transmitters in repair again, is now coming in. All this is a part of the life of Alaska, a part that was sorely missed when war restrictions silenced the hams.

Despite the foment and labor strife which still is sorely affecting Alaska shipping, the unsettled economy of the Territory, the difficulty in marketing agricultural products, bureaucratic remote controls—despite all this, as well as other handicaps common to a new and unsettled country, nothing on earth will keep Alaska from the development that her natural resources so richly merit. The Alaska Highway or some other highway eventually will furnish a year-round all-weather overland route to Alaska. Plans now are being aired for a railroad connection to the Territory, and a railroad extension from Fairbanks to the Arctic coast. Great continental and transcontinental air routes converge upon Alaska. New air lines recently have begun operating to and within the Territory. Plans for defense of the Americas now under way include a bulwark of bases throughout our far-flung northern territory—the bulwark that stopped Japan last time.

A word of warning from Alaska's eminent jurist and former congressional delegate, Judge Anthony Dimond, as quoted in the *Alaska Weekly*, should be given due consideration by all who plan to settle in Alaska: "I fear too many unfitted people are coming to Alaska now. Too many are coming who cannot live in Alaska and be happy here—too many who will not be able to understand anything except mosquitoes, cold, and the lack of sunshine."

But this and all other admonitions for caution will go unheeded by those who have fallen under Alaska's spell. Too many people now know too much of what Alaska has to offer. "For where else, under the American flag," they will ask, "are there such opportunities for individual success? And where else is free land for settlement? and tall straight spruce that may be cut free for the building of homes? and streams teeming with fish? and game in the near-by woods? and luscious wild berries everywhere? and the peacefulness and majesty of snow-capped mountains and huge glaciers? and flower-studded hills and valleys that give way in winter to snow-covered expanses for skiing and sledding? Where else can a man go to escape the noise and confusion and sameness of our humdrum struggle for existence, except to this land apart, this great rugged land—Alaska!"

Appendix

THE APPENDIX contains information, some of which is subject to change at any time, concerning exporting of game, game laws and bag limits, licenses; names and addresses of Alaska guides, the approximate time each has served, and the guide district each represents; game to be found in each guide district; fishing seasons, fur seasons, districts, etc. Also information relative to traveling costs, carriers, hotels; a list of Alaska air carriers; and the status of the Alaska Highway and other road and ferry connections.

This information is given so that the reader may obtain a general idea of these subjects. A copy of the current game regulations may be obtained from the Fish and Wildlife Service, Juneau, Alaska, and current highway information from the Alaska Road Commission, Juneau.

EXPORTING OF GAME

A licensed nonresident or alien is permitted to export during the respective open seasons not exceeding one deer, one moose, one caribou, one mountain goat, one mountain sheep, two in the aggregate of large brown and grizzly bears, not more than one of which shall have been taken either on the Kodiak-Afognak Island group or east of longitude 138 west, but not on both of said areas; three black bears, not more than two of which shall have been taken east of longitude 138 west; or not to exceed singly or in the aggregate one day's limit (10 birds) of grouse or ptarmigan.

GAME LAWS AND BAG LIMITS

(1) *Deer, bucks* (with horns not less than three inches above the top of the skull): East of longitude 138 west, September 1 to November 15. Limit: by a resident, two a season; by a nonresident, one a season. In the Prince William Sound drainage and near-by islands of southern Alaska, September 1 to September 30. Limit: one a season.

(2) *Moose, bulls* (except yearlings and calves): North of the Alaska Range, except in Colville River drainage, September 1 to September 20, and December 1 to December 7. Limit: one a year. South of the Alaska Range (but not in the Alaska No. 1 or Kenai No. 1 Peninsula areas nor in the Chilkoot and Chilkat River areas, nor in Yakutat Bay region between longitude 138 and 141 west) west of longitude 141 west, September 1 to 20, and December 15 to 21; east of longitude 138 west, September 15 to October 15. Limit: one a year.

(3) *Caribou* (except calves): In the Territory, but not in the area lying five miles on either side of the Steese Highway on Twelve Mile Summit between mileposts 84 and 89, and on Eagle Summit between milesposts 102 and 112, both districts lying northeast of Fairbanks in central Alaska, August 20 to September 30, and December 1 to 15. Limit: by resident, two a year; by nonresident, one a year.

(4) *Mountain goat* (except kids): In the Territory (but not in the Cooper Mountain area, Sheep Mountain area, Eklutna Lake area, Kenai Peninsula area No. 2, nor in the Girdwood area of Fur District 2, an area of approximately seventy-seven square miles near Anchorage in southern Alaska, nor on the Baranof and Chichagof Islands, nor in the watersheds of Tracy Arm, Endicott Arm, or Ford's Terror. all in southern Alaska and which are

closed), September 1 to October 31. Limit: by a resident, east of longitude 138 west, one a season; west of longitude 138 west, two a season; by a nonresident, one a season over entire Territory.

(5) *Mountain sheep, rams only* (except lambs): In the Territory, but not in the Cooper Mountain area, Kenai Peninsula Area No. 2, nor in the Girdwood, Sheep Mountain, and Eklutna areas. Limit: one ram a season.

(6) *Bear* (large, brown, and grizzly): East of longitude 138 west, but not in the Thayer Mountain and Pack Creek areas on Admiralty Island, and in the Kodiak-Afognak Island group, September 1 to June 20. Limit: one a year. In the rest of the Territory, September 1 to June 20. Limit: two a year.

(7) *Bear* (black, including its brown and blue, or glacier bear, color variations): East of longitude 138 west, including the Mount Hayes–Blair Lakes areas of southern and south central Alaska (but not in the Anan Creek and Loring areas of southeastern Alaska, which are closed), September 1 to June 20. Limit: two a season. In the rest of the Territory, no closed season. Limit: by a resident, no limit; by a nonresident, three a year. Black bear may not be taken at any place in the Territory within thirty-three feet of the middle of any highway.

(8) Any bear may be killed at any time or any place in the Territory when about to attack or molest persons or their property. Persons so killing such animals shall make a written report to the Commissioner, setting forth the reason for such killing and the time and place.

(9) *Hare and rabbit:* On the Kodiak-Afognak Island group, September 1 to March 31. No closed season in the rest of the Territory. No limit.

There is no closed season and no bag limit on wolf, coyote, wolverine, marmot, squirrel, and polar bear. For information concerning walrus and other large aquatic animals, inquiry should be addressed to the Fish and Wildlife Service, Juneau.

GAME BIRDS

Seasons and Bag Limits

(1) *Grouse and ptarmigan:* Except for certain closed areas which should be checked in current regulation, Fur Districts 1, 2, 3, 4, and 5, September 1 to February 28. Fur Districts 6, 7, and 8, August 20 to January 31. The bag limit is ten grouse, ten ptarmigan, or ten in the aggregate.

(2) *Game birds protected also under the provisions of the Migratory Bird Treaty Act:*

This group includes ducks, geese, and other migratory wild fowl covered by the above act. The season in Alaska is set each year, usually in September. Inquiry regarding season should be addressed to the Fish and Wildlife Service, Juneau, Alaska.

LICENSES

The nonresident general hunting, trapping, and game fishing license in Alaska is $50.00; hunting and fishing, not including big game, $10.00; game fishing, $2.50.

Resident license: trapping $3; hunting, $2; fishing, $1 (a trapping license includes the privilege of hunting and fishing; a hunting license includes the privilege of fishing); not required of native-born Indian or Eskimo, nor of resident under sixteen years of age. Export and return of trophies, $1 for each animal or bird. Export permit, if shipper is removing residence, $1 for each animal, $1 for each bird; if not removing residence, $5 for each animal, $1 for each bird.

Alien: special hunting, trapping, and fishing, $100.00; game fishing only, $2.50.

Licenses may be procured from licensing officers of the Alaska Game Commission located in all the principal towns of Alaska, or upon application to the Regional Office, Fish and Wildlife Service, Juneau, Alaska.

GUIDES

NAME	ADDRESS	APPROX. YEARS IN SERVICE	GUIDE DISTRICTS FOR WHICH LICENSED
Adams, John Q.	Anchorage	Over 5	1, 2, 3, 4
Anderson, Carl	Anchorage	Over 10	1, 2, 3, 4, 5, 6, 7, 8
Anderson, K. A.	Ketchikan	—	9
Berg, Emil	Kasilof	10	1, 2, 3, 4, 5, 6
Bishop, Geo. W.	Fairbanks	1	2, 6
Bolam, Alex	Moose Pass	Over 15	1, 2, 3, 4, 5, 6, 7, 8
Boyden, Henry	Nabesna	Over 15	3, 4, 5
Branham, E. T.	Anchorage	6	2, 3
Busby, Bob	Fairbanks	10	5, 6
Cannon, W. A.	P.O. Box 375 Kodiak	1	2, 3, 4
Chartrand, M. F.	P.O. Box 438 Anchorage	1	1, 2, 3, 4, 5
Chase, Will H.	Cordova	Over 20	1, 2, 3, 4, 5, 8
Collins, Grenold	Box 404 Anchorage	1	1, 2, 3, 4, 5, 6, 7, 8
Colvin, John	Healy Forks	Over 15	3, 4, 6
Cripe, Calvin	Fairbanks	Over 15	1, 2, 3, 4, 5, 6, 7, 8
Crosby, L. J.	P.O. Box 553 Juneau	1	9
Darden, W. L.	Anchorage	1	1, 2, 3, 4, 5, 6, 8
Dolan, James	Valdez	Over 10	1, 2, 3
Ellis, Lee S.	Wrangell	1	9
Elwell, Lewis M.	Anchorage	Over 15	1, 2, 3, 4, 5, 6, 7, 8
Gay, Ward I.	Anchorage	6	1, 2, 3, 4, 5
Hall, Ralph	Petersburg	1	9
Hancock, Lee	Anchorage	5	1, 2, 3, 4, 5, 6, 7, 8
Harris, F. B.	Juneau	—	9
Harris, John W.	Juneau	—	9

NAME	ADDRESS	APPROX. YEARS IN SERVICE	GUIDE DISTRICTS FOR WHICH LICENSED
Henton, Fred A.	Seward	Over 15	1, 2, 3, 4, 5, 6, 7, 8
Hersee, Ted	Homer	8	1, 2, 3, 4, 5
Horner, M. A.	Seward	Over 15	1, 2, 3, 4, 5, 6, 7, 8
Hunt, Wm. E.	Anchorage	2	1, 2, 3, 4, 5, 6
Jackson, W. H.	Box 1194 Ketchikan	1	9
Johnstone, Jack	Box 1227 Ketchikan	1	9
Judd, Fred C.	Anchorage	Over 15	1, 2, 3
Madsen, Alf	Kodiak	Over 15	1, 2, 3, 4, 5, 6, 7, 8
Mallot, Jay B.	Yakutat	—	Yakutat area in upper southeastern Alaska
Metrokin, Eli	Kodiak	Over 15	1, 2, 3, 4, 5, 6, 7, 8
Moore, M. W.	Box 785 Ketchikan	15	1, 2, 3, 4, 5, 6, 7, 8
Moore, Tom A.	Box 1457 Anchorage	4	1, 2, 3, 4, 5, 6
Morgan, Victor	Anchorage	6	1, 2, 3, 4, 5, 6, 7, 8
Mossburg, W. F.	Box 1441 Ketchikan	1	9
Myers, Wesley	Box 1516 Ketchikan	Over 15	9
Nelson, Geo. B.	Coopers Landing	Over 15	1, 2, 3, 4, 5, 6
Oberg, Oscar	Juneau	Over 15	9
O'Dale, Tom	Anchorage	Over 20	1, 2, 3, 4, 5, 6, 7, 8
Parker, E. W.	Anchorage	6	3
Pennington, L. L.	Anchorage	2	2, 3
Peterson, A. L.	Unga	Over 15	1, 2, 3, 4, 5, 6
Philbin, D. O.	Petersburg	—	9

NAME	ADDRESS	APPROX. YEARS IN SERVICE	GUIDE DISTRICTS FOR WHICH LICENSED
Reischl, R. A.	Juneau	Over 15	9
Revell, Frank S.	Lakeview	Over 15	1, 2, 3, 4, 5, 6, 7, 8
Rising, F. W.	Anchorage	Over 10	1, 2, 3, 4, 5, 6
Shellabarger, Max	Skwentna via Anchorage	8	1, 3, 4, 7
Simons, A. A.	Lakeview via Seward	Over 20	1, 2, 3, 4, 5, 6, 7, 8
Stringer, E. L.	Petersburg	1	9
Thompson, F. S.	Box 2152 Anchorage	1	4, 5; asst. 1, 2, 8
Tousley, C. C.	Anchorage	Over 15	1, 2, 3, 4, 5
Vogel, Oscar H.	Anchorage	10	1, 2, 3, 4
Warren, Jack	Fairbanks	10	1, 2, 3, 4, 5, 6, 7, 8
Wilkins, Warren M.	Ketchikan	Over 5	9
Wilkins, W. M.	CAA Section 55 Anchorage	1	1, 2, 3, 8
Wooton, Frank J.	Petersburg	1	9
Wooton, Ralph E.	Petersburg	10	9

It should be mentioned that the length of service given in the foregoing list may, but does not necessarily, imply that the long-service guide is more proficient than one of a shorter service. The Game Commission regularly urges some excellent prospective guides to enter the service, and some of them from time to time accede to the urging and enter the service. The length of service is given as information for the prospective hunter, as it stands to reason that the long-service guide is likely still to be in service two, three, or even five years from now; and available for information to help the prospective hunter plan his trip. The length of service of five guides was not available at the time this list was compiled and is for that reason left blank.

If none of the regular guides listed above are available for the area at the time the prospective hunter wishes to plan his hunting trip, a temporary guide that can qualify may be appointed by the Game Commission upon application.

Below is a list of game animals to be found in each guide district. It must be understood that there is some overlapping of different species, and the lists given here cover the predominant species in each guide district.

Guide District 1, Kenai Peninsula area of southern Alaska: moose, mountain sheep, brown, grizzly, and black bear, and mountain goat.

Guide District 2, Alaska Peninsula–Kodiak area of southwestern Alaska: brown and grizzly bear, moose, and caribou.

Guide District 3, Cook Inlet–Rainey Pass area of south-southwestern Alaska: brown, grizzly, and black bear, sheep in limited numbers, moose, and caribou.

Guide District 4, Chicaloon-Nelchina area of south central Alaska: mountain sheep, grizzly and black bear (including the glacier bear subspecies), mountain goat, caribou, and moose.

Guide District 5, Copper and White River areas of southern and south central Alaska: mountain sheep, caribou, moose, mountain goat, large brown, grizzly, and black bear (including the glacier bear subspecies).

Guide District 6, Fairbanks–Upper Tenana area of central Alaska: mountain sheep, caribou, moose, grizzly and black bear.

Guide District 7, Kuskokwim district of southwestern Alaska: mountain sheep, caribou, moose, grizzly and black bear.

Guide District 8, Arctic, northern Alaska: caribou, moose, mountain sheep, grizzly and black bear, and polar bear on the Arctic seacoast.

Guide district 9, southeastern Alaska: brown, grizzly, and black bears (including the glacier bear subspecies), mountain goats, Sitkan black-tailed deer, and an occasional moose in certain mainland river valleys.

With the information contained in Chapter 2, Hunting, concerning Alaska's big game animals, their desirability and distribution, and with the outline of seasons, bag limits, licenses, registered guides with their addresses and the guide district each represents, and the different species of game animals to be found in each guide district outlined in the Appendix, the prospective hunter should be in position to plan his Alaska hunt and should be able to consummate his arrangements with a minimum of correspondence and delay.

OUTLINE OF FUR DISTRICTS, SEASONS, AND LICENSES *

Fur Districts:

Fur District 1: southeastern Alaska, east of longitude 138.

Fur District 2: practically the whole of southern Alaska.

Fur District 3: southwestern Alaska and the Aleutian islands.

Fur District 4: Bristol Bay area of western Alaska.

Fur District 5: Kuskokwim Bay region of western Alaska.

Fur District 6: watershed of Tanana River, upper Copper River, and part of the lower Yukon and upper Kuskokwim.

Fur District 7: drainage of upper Koyukuk and upper Yukon rivers.

Fur District 8: the Arctic Coast.

Seasons on mink, land otter, weasel (ermine), fox, and lynx:

Fur District 1: December 16 to January 15, except there shall be no open season on mink. No limit.

* Where no district or season is listed on certain fur bearers there is no open season at present.

Fur District 2: November 16 to January 15, except there shall be no open season on white and blue foxes. No limit.

Fur District 3: December 1 to February 28. No limit.

Fur District 4: November 16 to February 15. No limit.

Fur District 5: November 16 to February 28. No limit.

St. Lawrence Island Eskimo Reservation: white fox season, December 16 to March 15. No limit.

Fur Districts 6 and 7: November 16 to February 28. No limit.

Fur District 8: December 1 to March 31. No limit.

Seasons on muskrat:

Fur Districts 1 and 2: April 1 to May 31. No limit.

Fur Districts 3 and 4: March 10 to May 10, except there shall be no open season on the Kodiak–Afognak Island group. No limit.

Fur District 5: North of Unalakleet River drainage, April 1 to June 7. Unalakleet River drainage and south thereof, April 1 to May 31. No limit.

Fur Districts 6 and 7: March 1 to May 31. No limit.

Fur District 8: April 10 to June 10. No limit.

Seasons on beaver:

Fur District 1: April 1 to April 30. Limit: ten a season.

Fur District 2: February 1 to March 31, except there shall be no open season on a strip one-half mile wide on either side of the Alaska Railroad, nor on the Kenai Peninsula south of Kenai River, Kenai Lake, and Skilak Lake. Limit: ten a season.

Fur District 5: February 1 to March 31. Limit: ten a season.

Fur District 6: February 1 to March 31, except there shall be no open season on a strip one-half mile on either side of the Alaska Railroad, nor within the Tanana River drainage east of the Richardson Highway from Richardson Monument (202 miles from Valdez) to Big Delta (280 miles from Valdez), nor south and east of the Goodpaster River drainage, nor within the Fairbanks area. Limit: ten a season.

Fur District 7: February 1 to March 31. Limit: ten a season.

*Wolf, coyote, wolverine, marmot, squirrel, and polar
    bear:*
All fur districts: no closed season. No limit.

Seasons on marten:
Fur District 1: December 16 to January 5, except there shall be
no open season on Prince of Wales Island. Limit: twenty a season.
Fur Districts 2, 3, 4, 5, 6, and 7: November 16 to January 31.
Limit: thirty a season.

No skins of beavers or martens, whether taken within or
without the Territory, shall be possessed or transported by
any person until the same have been sealed with a seal pre-
scribed by the Commission, except that persons taking
beavers or martens within the Territory may possess the unsealed skins thereof, during the open season therefor and for
30 days thereafter, and within the same period may transport
the same unsealed for the purpose of having them sealed or
tagged by a wildlife agent or other officer authorized by the
Commission.
Also when skins of fur animals or black bears are shipped out of
the Territory, the shipper is required to furnish the transportation
agent a statement showing the number of skins, and declaring that
no illegal skin or unsealed beaver skin is contained in the shipment.
If the skins are taken out of the Territory, a like statement must
be furnished the collector of customs at the port of clearance.

Note: Newspaper releases, as this goes to press, indicate a
temporary closed season on mink throughout the Territory.
Also a shortening of the season on marten in southeastern Alaska
to January 5 and a limit of twenty to each trapper.

Licenses:
Resident (one who has resided in the Territory for a continuous period of three years immediately preceding): trapping, $3
(includes hunting and fishing).

Nonresident: $50 (includes hunting and fishing).
Alien: $100 (includes hunting and fishing).
Fur Farm: $2.
Fur Dealer: resident, $10; nonresident, $100; alien, $500. Resident agent, $10; nonresident agent, $100; alien agent, $500.

Bounties on wolves and coyotes:
Bounties on wolves and coyotes are now $30 on wolves and $25 on coyotes.

GAME FISHES

Creel Limits, Fishing Licenses, and Seasons
Rainbow, steelhead, cutthroat, eastern brook, and Dolly Varden trout, Mackinaw or lake trout, and grayling: June 5 to September 30 on the Buskin River and Buskin Lake near Kodiak, Kenai River and all lakes and tributaries thereof; June 1 to September 30 on Dewey Lake near Skagway and Salmon Creek Reservoir near Juneau; rest of Territory, no closed season. Limits: throughout most of the Territory—twenty fishes singly or in the aggregate, but not to exceed fifteen pounds and one fish daily, two daily bag limits in possession. Check limits and seasons at time of trip as minor changes often occur.

In salt water throughout the Territory and in lakes and streams west of Cook Inlet, including such as are designated above but excepting the Nome and Snake Rivers on Seward Peninsula, there shall be no limit on Dolly Varden trout.

Licenses:
Resident, $1; nonresident and alien, $2.50. A fishing license is included with each hunting license.

TRAVELING COSTS AND CARRIERS

Steamship fares from Seattle to Alaska points at present in round figures are as follows: Ketchikan, $39; Wrangell, $42;

Petersburg, $47; Juneau, $51; Sitka, Haines, and Skagway, $59; Cordova, $88; Seward, $94; Kodiak, $111; and other near-by towns not listed carry approximately the same rates. Half fares are required for children five to twelve, with a meal charge for children two to four. These fares include meals. Round-trip fares are double the one way. At present, taxes of approximately 30 per cent must be added.

Airplane fares are about 65 per cent higher than boat fares, but are expected to be reduced to somewhere near steamship rates within a few years.

Reservations, especially boat reservations, should be made two weeks or more in advance of expected sailings.

For convenience of Alaska-bound travelers from the north central portions of the United States, a round trip is available from Minneapolis–St. Paul, with a ninety-day limit, by way of Canadian Pacific Railroad to Vancouver, connecting with their steamship line at that point. The round-trip fare to Vancouver is $107.95 plus tax. Steamship fares from Vancouver to Alaska points are slightly less than from Seattle. It is also possible and very feasible to go by uncrowded Canadian National Railroad from Chicago and the east coast to Prince Rupert, B. C., and thence by boat over the very short hundred miles to Ketchikan or to other more distant southeastern Alaska ports. The round trip from New York, including Pullman, is $221. The railroad fare only from St. Paul is $117.68 for the round trip.

Steamship lines serving the Territory from Seattle are the Alaska Steamship Company, Northland Transportation Company, and Alaska Transportation Company; Canadian Pacific maintains service from Seattle, Victoria, and Vancouver to southeastern Alaska points. Canadian National has service from Vancouver to Ketchikan.

Pan-American and Northwest Airlines have regular service from the States to Alaska points.

Inquiry for information concerning rates to more distant Alaska points should be addressed to one or more of the above carriers.

Travelers from the central and southern portions of the United States will be amazed at the higher cost of services prevailing throughout interior Alaska. A haircut costs from $1.00 to $1.25; shave 75¢. Ham and eggs cost 85¢ to $1.00, and meals in the roadhouses along the highways usually are served at a flat price of $1.50 per person for either breakfast, lunch, or dinner. A bowl of chili or a hamburger costs 35¢ to 50¢.

Laundry work is out of all proportion throughout most of Alaska. A charge of 40¢ for shirts, 25¢ for shorts, 20¢ for short undershirts, 15¢ for socks, and 60¢ for pajama suits is from a laundry in central Alaska. The prices are somewhat lower in southeastern Alaska.

Hotel rates are in line with those prevailing in good hotels in the States, from $4.00 to $6.00 a day for two people. Roadhouses and hunting lodges also charge $4.00 to $6.00 a day, exclusive of meals.

If a traveler has his own sleeping facilities, and buys and prepares his own food and does his own laundry work when traveling in Alaska, his costs will probably run 25 to 30 per cent higher than in the States.

Roadhouses are available along Alaska's highways, usually within a hundred miles of each other, sometimes within only a few miles, where accommodations of varying degrees of comfort and convenience may be had. Hotels are available in all of the principal towns. Owing to the influx of travelers and settlers, all accommodations are badly overcrowded, and it will be well for anyone contemplating a trip to Alaska to postpone it until inquiry reveals a letup in the travel situation or until more accommodations may be provided; or be prepared to sleep outside in weather where excessive rainfall is a certainty and where the temperature in summer is in the neighborhood of 50. This suggestion should not be taken lightly. Ketchikan and other entrance towns are resorting to many expedients such as tent camps to alleviate the inconvenience occasioned by the present shortage.

Gasoline usually is available at nearly all roadhouses along the highways, but it is well for the traveler to keep his tank near the full mark as occasional shortages occur. Gasoline costs 22¢ to 25¢ per gallon in the larger towns along the coast, but the price along the highways is 35¢ to 50¢, and varies considerably in the inland towns—from 26¢ to 35¢. Tire services, including fixing punctures, vulcanizing, etc., average about twice the charge for similar services in the States.

To ship one's car from Seattle to Valdez costs approximately $200 one way, and a ninety-day trip by car from the central portion of the United States to the coast, thence to Valdez by boat and throughout Alaska by car, costs in the neighborhood of $2,000 for two people, including meals and accommodations at the better grade hotels and roadhouses. This includes return costs to the traveler's home in the States. It will allow him about sixty days within the Territory.

HOTELS

For the convenience of those who wish to make hotel reservations in Alaska, a list of hotels is given below.

Anchorage: Anchorage Hotel, Lane Hotel, Lido Hotel, Parsons Hotel, Rainy Pass Lodge, Westward Hotel.

Cordova: Northern Hotel, Windsor Hotel, Alaskan Hotel, Manhattan Hotel.

Fairbanks: Arctic Hotel, DeLuxe Hotel, Fairbanks Hotel, Fairview Hotel, International Hotel, Nordale Hotel, Lacy Street Hotel, Northern Hotel, Pioneer Hotel and Bar, Savoy Hotel and Bar, Steel Hotel.

Juneau: Baranof Hotel, Gastineau Hotel, Juneau Hotel, Northern Hotel, and small hotels and rooming houses too numerous to mention.

Ketchikan: Alaska Hotel, Gilmore Hotel, Ingersoll Hotel, Marine Hotel, Stedman Hotel, Rex Hotel. Near Ketchikan, reached by mail boat, is Bell Isle, partly modern and soon expected to be completely modernized.

Kodiak: Sunbeam Hotel.

Nome: Lincoln Hotel and Bar, Polar Rooms, Wallace Hotel.

Palmer: Co-op Dormitory, Felton House.

Petersburg: Arctic Hotel.

Seward: New Seward Hotel, Palace Hotel, Van Gilder Hotel, Spokane Rooms and Apartments.

Sitka: Alaska Hotel, Bay View Hotel, Sitka Hotel.

Skagway: Pullen House.

Valdez: Golden North Hotel, Valdez Hotel, Annex Hotel.

Wrangell: Wrangell Hotel.

Visitors should inquire at entrance towns regarding roadhouses, as many old ones are in the process of modernization, and many new ones are under construction.

ALASKA AIR CARRIERS

For the convenience of those that may wish to make reservations for a trip by air anywhere within Alaska, following is a current list giving the names of Alaska Air Carriers with their addresses:

AHO Flying Service, Anchorage

Alaska Airlines, Anchorage

Alaska Coastal Airlines, Juneau

Armstrong Air Service, Dillingham

Arctic Airways, Candle

Brennon Flying Service, Manly Springs

Bristol Bay Air Service, Anchorage

Brown Flying Service, Bethel

Christensen Air Service, Anchorage
Collins, Grenold, Anchorage
Cordova Air Service, Dillingham
Dodson Air Service, Fairbanks
Ellis Air Transport, Ketchikan
Ferguson Airways, Kotzebue
Gillam Airways, Fairbanks
Jones Airways, Bethel
Ketchikan Air Service, Ketchikan
Laverty, Wm. L., Anchorage
Martin, Carl E., Anchorage
Morgan, Myron S., Aleknagik
Munz Air Service, Nome
McDonald, Philip, McGrath
Nicholson Air Service, Dillingham
Northern Air Service, Fairbanks
Pan-American Airways (principal towns)
Petersburg Air Service, Petersburg
Petersburg Flying Service, Anchorage
Toussaint, E. A., Fort Yukon
Walatka Air Service, Dillingham
Wein Alaska Airways, Fairbanks
Winchell, Oscar, Anchorage
Woodley Airways, Anchorage
Wren, Donald, Aleknagik

Information relative to pilot requirements or air-line possibilities in Alaska may be obtained from Mr. E. Putman, Chief Administrator, Civil Aeronautics, Anchorage, Alaska.

ALASKA HIGHWAY, HAINES CUTOFF, AND FERRY ROUTES

The Alaska Highway was built as an emergency military road, and it extends from its connection with the Richardson Highway near Fairbanks some 1,500 miles in a southeasterly direction to the railhead at Dawson Creek in Canada. There is no all-weather road connection between the Dawson Creek end of the highway and the States. Canada has assumed complete control of that portion of the highway within her border and has made preparations to improve it. Canada is also working on a connecting road to the States calling for completion in 1947. Thus it would be wise to eliminate it as a possibility for travelers until the summer of 1948, and inquiry should be made at that time relative to travel conditions over the highway.

The Haines Cutoff, which is a short cut from the Alaska highway to the coast at the town of Haines, has been closed in recent months for repairs, and nothing definite has developed relative to its permanent maintenance. Inquiry should also be made concerning the use of this highway before attempting it.

A ferry service from Canadian ports to Haines is under consideration and its operation will depend upon the status of the highway connection at that point.